D1177647

THE BACK TO COOKING COOKBOOK

THE
BACK
TO
COOKING
COOKBOOK

By Ceil Dyer

Illustrated by Mary Means

PRICE STERN SLOAN *publishers,* INC.

LOS ANGELES

DEDICATION

To the Modern American Home Food Industry and its hard working publicists, without whose untiring efforts we would never have had so many great Italian, French and Chinese restaurants in this wonderful country.

CONTENTS

THE BACK TO COOKING COOKBOOK

The French maintain that American cuisine is based on canned soup.

It's fast becoming a fact. It's a safe bet to say that at least ninety percent of the recipes in newspaper food columns across the country are written by large food companies, and at least seventy-five percent dreamed up by women's magazine food editors are designed to appease advertisers. It's no wonder that almost all instructions for preparing these "new" recipes begin with "Take two boxes - cartons - or cans" - and it's no wonder indeed that the average woman has forgotten (or never learned) how to cook such simple basics as soups, sauces and stews.

She has been brainwashed. Really, it's a crime!

Today's high cost of food is not nearly so much the result of an increase in prices at the supermarket as it is a decrease in intelligent buying.

Shopping carts are filled for the most part with cake mixes, icing mixes, bottled salad dressing, packaged cookies, "instant" rice, no-cook puddings, canned sauces, and soups, soups, and more soups. These last to be used as a base for every conceivable dish.

Prices may be bemoaned, but necessity is never questioned. The poor shopper has been mesmerized into believing that these so-called "convenience" foods are "smart buys" and "modern" staple items that will miraculously save her money - as well as effort and time.

The truth, of course, is exactly the reverse. Home cooked meals made from honest ingredients are far less expensive, taste better and are more nutritious than those made from ersatz concoctions. What is more, they need take no more time to prepare than mixing and matching pre-cooked, canned, bottled, packaged, dehydrated and frozen foods.

This simple fact, however, has been buried under reams of slick magazine and newspaper copy, folksy food articles and a steady stream of never-ceasing television and radio commercials.

Unfortunately, money plus the good wholesome flavor of honest food minus preservatives is not all that is lost. An alarming number of Americans are both overweight and undernourished, the direct result—according to both doctors and nutritionists—of too many fatty, starchy foods and not enough protein. Lack of integrity on the part of the food manufacturers, processors, and packers, their public relations counsellors, and advertising agencies can certainly be blamed, at least in good part.

TV dinners are inadequate meals, no matter how attractively packaged. Canned soups are not, in spite of the glowing all-color, full-page magazine advertisements, as nutritious or even one-half as good as mother used to make (even if she was only a reasonably good cook)... and no matter how healthy looking that young man on the new color screen in your living room looks, the packaged cereal that he appears to be eating with such relish does not provide "all the necessary body-building protein and energy needed each day for an active, growing boy." Nor does that whipped-up pudding shown in the very next commercial resemble in any way custard made at home from fresh whole eggs and cream.

It really does seem incredible! Sensible, hard-working, down to earth America is being "conned" and in a big way.

Though "Mammoth Foods" stock may be a good buy on the "big board," the mix and match product it sells assuredly is not --- and it's the consumer who's left with a slim purse, holding the very light bag.

Surely something should be done. If only just a few of the basic facts of good food plus the simple A.B.C.'s of nutrition were brought forth - if "home-made" were honestly compared as to flavor, labor and cost against condensed, dehydrated, frozen and precooked - the tide might at least in some part be reversed.

If shoppers would erase these products from their lists, food budgets could be reduced by an easy one third. What's more, nourishing meals would once again appear on American tables and the pleasure of dining, not just eating from hunger, might be regained ... something worth fighting for in this rush and hurry world when gracious living is rapidly becoming a thing of the past.

All costs and comparisons are based upon New York markets, Spring 1969. Though prices vary throughout the country, the proportionate savings as shown in this book will remain approximately the same.

WHAT "GOES" WITH SALADS

WHAT "GOES" WITH SALADS

Select a small but attractive bottle of low calorie dressing from the diet food counter of your favorite department store (cost, from 49 to 79 cents per 8 ounce bottle depending upon style of bottle and brand). Pick up, and pay for, naturally, one small tube of cement glue for about 35 cents and approximately one dollar's worth of colorful sequins (or pellets) of the type elderly ladies are prone to sew on baby pink or pastel blue nylon cardigan sweaters.

Now hurry along home and, setting aside the sequins (or pellets) and glue, plunge the unopened bottle of dressing directly into a large pan of very hot water; soak until all paper may be easily removed and discarded. Before discarding, however, take note of the contents in your bottle - you will usually find a list of ingredients in small type on the back label that should read something like this: vegetable oil, vinegar, egg yolk, salt, gum tragacanth, sufficient water to prepare, sorbic acid, cyclamate sodium, a non-nutritive artificial sweetner which should be used by persons who must restrict their intake of ordinary sweets, and U.S. certified food coloring, B. H. A., propyl gallate and calcium disodium E.D.T.A., added to maintain freshness. (From the label of a bottle of diet dressing put out by a major food company specializing in diet foods.)

If you are satisfied that your particular purchase contains nothing harmful to your drainpipe, open the bottle and pour the contents down the drain - rinse and blot the bottle dry. Place it on a large sheet of old newspaper and with a small paint brush, completely cover the entire surface with a thin film of glue. Now, holding it up by the lip (top opening) with your right index finger, carefully sprinkle (using your left hand) glue with a bright and glittering covering of sequins or pellets - isn't this fun!! (We stole the entire idea from an old Christmas issue of "Woman's Home Day".) Press sequins firmly into glue with the tips of your fingers, and voila! There you are! A lovely bud vase or a whatnot (?) for a whatnot stand or table, and a perfect birthday gift for Aunt Agatha or for that matter, anyone else you also actively dislike.

On second thought (maybe it should have been our first), perhaps it would be wise to forget the whole thing from start to finish and simply take a brisk walk. Aunt Agatha will be just as offended by no gift as a useless one in poor taste. While walking, use the money instead to purchase a large bottle of pure vegetable oil to which no preservatives have been added (peanut or olive oil for example), and a bottle of fine, imported French wine vinegar of an equally large size. You'll have ample change left over to buy a small pepper grinder, if you don't already own one, and a bottle of peppercorns to use in it. Ingredients for homemade dressing that will taste even better than that French dressing made just for you by that handsome young waiter in Paris last year (or for that matter when and where-ever you last had such a treat). What's more, portion for portion, it will cost far less than that ersatz concoction we hope you had sense enough to refrain from buying at all. In fact and indeed, it will also cost less and taste better and be better for your health than any kind of prepared bottled dressing.

As to the difference in calories, and we admit they are great (approximately 42 calories in one teaspoon of homemade dressing, only six to nine in each teaspoon of its bottled diet substitute), you need them, no matter what your weight. To prove it, we quote from Adele Davis, nutritionist, A.B., M.S., author of Let's Eat Right To Keep Fit.

"For three reasons, eating too little fat is a major cause of overweight. First, many seemingly fat persons are only waterlogged. An adequate diet including salad oil daily, often causes them to lose pounds.

"Second, when the essential fatty acids* are insufficiently supplied, the body changes sugar into fat much more rapidly than is normal. This quick change makes the blood sugar plunge downward, causing you to be starved as a wolf. The chances are you will overeat and gain weight.

"Third, fats are more satisfying than any other foods. If you forego eating 100 calories of fat per meal, you usually become so hungry that you eat 500 calories of starch and/or sugar simply because you cannot resist them. Unwanted pounds creep on. If you want to maintain your weight or reduce, eat at least two tablespoons of fat daily."

*A principal source - natural vegetable oil.

We hope you're convinced. Life is so much more pleasant with good food and good health. A great salad, great tasting, great for you, is a liberal helping of both.

The money saved by preparing your own homemade dressing is only a bonus, though a hearty one when you total the facts.

Prepared French dressing, eight ounce bottle (one cup) costs 39 to 89 cents and up. Contents: Oil, vinegar, spices, and preservatives. Honestly, that's all; read the labels! What you are paying for, says the maker, is his "superb" blending plus his "magical" touch.

French dressing made at home: Cost depends on the type of oil and vinegar, however, it can come to no more than 24 cents based on one cup of oil from best quality pure peanut oil at 80 cents a quart, plus ¼ cup best quality imported French wine vinegar at 60 cents per quart, and seasoning: salt, sugar and black Java pepper.

How much time does it take to save this much money? Something like two minutes or less.

BASIC FRENCH DRESSING

(1¼ cups)

1   teaspoon salt
¾   teaspoon coarse ground black pepper
¼   teaspoon sugar
¼   cup vinegar
1   cup oil

Add salt, pepper and sugar to vinegar. Mix well, add oil, beat lightly, then beat once again just before adding to salad. Can be mixed in a bottle, covered, shaken well and stored in the refrigerator to be used as needed. One fourth cup is ample for four servings of salad.

If you prefer a more interesting dressing to classic French, there is still no need to get carried away by a label. Such "exotics" as Sherry wine dressing, Roquefort cheese dressing, creamy French, Thousand Island, and Italian can range in price from 59 cents to well over a dollar for an eight ounce bottle. Make your own. The savings again are substantial and the fresh flavor is always a vast improvement to the knowledgeable palate.

CREAMY FRENCH DRESSING

To 1¼ cups basic French dressing, add one egg yolk to vinegar and blend well before adding oil. Beat with wire whisk until smooth, or blend in electric blender for five seconds.

Approximate cost: 30 cents. Standard brand eight ounce bottle (one cup) costs: 49 cents.

ROQUEFORT CHEESE DRESSING

To 1¼ cups basic French dressing, add one egg yolk to vinegar before adding oil, blend well. Add oil and crumble in ¼ cup Roquefort cheese. Whirl in blender or beat well with wire whisk. Approximate cost: 65 cents. Gourmet type bottle with real Roquefort cheese costs: 69 cents.

GARLIC FRENCH DRESSING

Drop one small clove of garlic into basic French dressing, let mellow a few hours before serving. Approximate cost: 25 cents (1¼ cups). Standard brand eight ounce bottle (one cup) costs: 49 cents.

HERB FRENCH DRESSING

To 1¼ cups basic French dressing, add 1 teaspoon finely chopped parsley, ¼ teaspoon dry mustard, ½ teaspoon each basil and tarragon. Pour dressing into a bottle and shake, but like crazy, or go the route of the electric blender. Approximate cost: 30 cents for 1¼ cups. Standard brand eight ounce bottle (one cup) costs: 49 cents.

FRENCH THOUSAND ISLAND DRESSING

To 1¼ cups basic French dressing, add one tablespoon each finely chopped green pepper, pimiento, stuffed green olives sweet pickles and capers. You may also add, if desired, a generous dash of Tabasco and ½ teaspoon Worchestershire sauce. Approximate cost: 35 cents (1½ cups). Standard brand eight ounce bottle (one cup) costs: 69 cents.

ITALIAN DRESSING

Substitute olive oil for corn oil in basic French dressing recipe. Add one split clove of garlic, let dressing mellow in refrigerator two hours or more. Shake or beat well just before using. Approximate cost: 25 cents for 1¼ cups. Standard brand eight ounce bottle (one cup) costs: 59 cents. For a fresh and light flavor, you may also substitute all or part fresh lemon juice for vinegar.

MAYONNAISE

Blender made it takes no time at all - but by hand it's still not nearly as difficult as you may have been led to believe. The effort? Well worth your time. As to the flavor, any so-called gourmet will tell you it's worth twice the price of "Commercially Made," but again, of course, it costs less. Real mayonnaise in a jar, eight ounces (one cup): 39 cents. Mayonnaise homemade, about 1¼ cups: 30 cents.

MAYONNAISE
(1¼ cups)

½	teaspoon salt
½	teaspoon sugar
2	egg yolks
2	teaspoons lemon juice (or white wine vinegar)
1	cup salad oil

Mix salt and sugar with egg yolks, add one tablespoon lemon juice, blend to a paste, add oil in a thin steady stream, beating continuously with a rotary beater (or at medium speed in an electric blender). As it thickens, add second tablespoon lemon juice and continue beating until stiff.

RUSSIAN DRESSING

Add to 1¼ cups mayonnaise, two teaspoons each chili sauce, finely chopped pimientos, green pepper, and sweet pickles, one tablespoon fresh lemon juice and chopped chives.

You can also add to freshly made mayonnaise, diced or grated Swiss, blue or American cheese, shrimp or crabmeat, mixed, cooked and chopped vegetables, grated orange rind, chopped chives, anchovies or capers, tomato catsup, Tabasco sauce or tomato paste. In other words, you can flavor to taste. It's up to you and what goes in your salad.

If all this seems like too too much trouble, let's face it, you really are lazy, but still there's no need to return to the bottle. Prepare your greens, pour in oil, toss well, add vinegar, salt and spices and toss again. Now honestly, are two bottles more work than one? Just be brave about the seasoning, and remember you have to "toss" even with "already prepared" dressing.

To salad greens for four to six portions of salad, use three tablespoons oil, one tablespoon vinegar, one teaspoon salt, ¼ teaspoon coarse ground black pepper and ¼ teaspoon sugar (optional but good).

You can vary the taste of your salad by adding to any combination of greens; leaf or head lettuce, spinach, romaine, escarole, chicory or watercress; or whatever else you find crisp and fresh in your market: paper thin slices of green pepper, chopped chives, fresh chopped basil and tarragon, young nasturtium leaves, as well as chopped anchovies, slivers of Swiss cheese, Virginia ham, crumbled blue or Roquefort cheese, chopped sweet pickles, diced fresh pear or peaches, celery seed, diced cucumber, chutney (Major Grey variety), avocado, purple onion rings, citrus fruit, sliced raw mushrooms and so on ad infinitum.

You may also use olive oil in place of corn oil, peanut oil in place of olive oil, fresh lemon juice instead of vinegar, red wine vinegar in place of white, etc., etc., and etc.

In fact, you can mix and match to *your* taste, not that of the guy who puts it up to make a neat profit in a bottle.

SALAD DRESSING [MIX] NOT FOR BUYING

(Someone out there, in the home food industry, likes gullible, insecure, "in the kitchen" little you. You're so profitable.)

Dehydrated in a package - cost about 20 cents. Here's a perfect example of how Mrs. John Q. Public is taken, once again, by the American food industry know-how. And boy, do they know how.

Packaged dehydrated salad dressing mixes (you add oil, vinegar and water) are absolutely unnecessary products. They detract from, do not add to, the good flavor of salads.

They have no nutritional value. If you are insecure about properly seasoning a salad - don't.

Rely on the best and freshest tender young vegetables and greens, unbruised and perfect. Add bland oil, toss; add salt, toss; add the finest French wine vinegar you can afford, toss again and serve. (See preceding instructions for proportions.) The vinegar is pre-seasoned; so are the vegetables.

You do not need:
Dehydrated onion salad dressing mix.

If you want an oniony salad, add a few chopped, fresh

scallions or chives to the salad, not the dressing, and proceed as above. Your salad will taste far better than if tossed with a dressing made with dehydrated onions, water, algin derivative, sodium phosphate and acetyltartrate mono and diglycerides, among other things. The savings effected will be about 16 cents if you use, say about four tablespoons or four cents worth of chopped chives or scallions. Could they cost more?*

You do not need:

Dehydrated Italian style salad dressing mix.

If you want an Italian style salad, use pure virgin olive oil, the best from Italy, and add one clove garlic to basic oil and vinegar dressing (see preceding instructions). Though the Italians do use many spices and seasoning in their cuisine, they do not add them to salad dressing. Intelligent and rational people, they know when enough is too much. Not so the makers of Italian salad dressing mixes. Besides preservatives, they add almost everything ever found in an Italian kitchen with the exception of the dehydrated tail of a Roman cat.

You do not need:

French salad dressing mix.

One maker of this product labels his shiny little package "old-fashioned French salad dressing mix." Much thought was put into this title. The "old-fashioned" adds

---

* Salad dressing mixes are made for and bought by the same people who, because they are unsure of their own mixability, buy bottled martinis. We wonder if these are the same people who buy pre-tied bow ties, and order their flowers arranged by the florist? How too sad. Besides the money wasted, think of the fun they miss.

a "homey," "folksy" touch to what otherwise might be considered exotic and "too foreign tasting" by the midwestern market, or so he was told by his Eastern advertising agency. But really, nothing could be less exotic than authentic French dressing. The French feel very much as the Italians about salads, only more so. Garlic is rarely used. They rely instead on tender young greens and more often than not, nothing else, washed, then thoroughly dried, leaf by leaf before being tossed with plain oil and vinegar. Water in a salad dressing, mon Dieu! Escoffier would rise from his grave.

CHEESE SPREADS
AND
OTHER BEGINNINGS

CHEESE SPREADS
AND OTHER BEGINNINGS

Take four (8 oz.) jars of pasteurized process CHEESE food spread, wrap each one individually in heavy duty foil and place in a plastic (or other water and moisture proof) bag. Stuff additional crumbled foil between each jar (absolutely eliminating any chance of breakage), seal the bag with Scotch tape and pack it away with your other Safari gear. You do have your Safari gear, don't you? After all, one never knows just when one will be invited to jet along for a swing at a shoot, now does one?

The reason for taking along the pasteurized process CHEESE food spread? Well, you just might not find it readily available in Africa or wherever, and it's a positive must out there on those hot dusty plains. Because, if you are not going to let that beastly heat utterly destroy your complexion, you simply have got to have lots and lots of moisture to replace that lost by dehydration from hot winds and sun. Pasteurized process CHEESE food spread has it! And in abundance.

In fact there is from 40 to 60 percent real, honest to goodness moisture in each little eight-ounce jar. Now, isn't that great? It's the sensible way to take along what you need without excess charges for overweight on the plane. Besides, it's non-alcoholic as well. .In fact, it's also practically non-everything else. Non-natural cheese flavor, for instance.

When you pasteurize and process cheese you heat it to a temperature of 150° F. (or over) and then just let it bubble away until it's positively sterile (ghastly word that). And this, of course, just boils away almost all the natural flavor, which really shouldn't concern us anyway because pasteurized process CHEESE food spread is practically non-cheese in the first place. What we mean is it's PROCESSED, not processed-finished, as in the language of office procedure big business, but processed, "added to," as in the language of big business food: though the results are practically one and the same when it comes to cheese in pasteurized processed CHEESE food spread. Why? I'll tell you why. It's because the makers substitute such things as dry skim milk powder, whey, sodium phosphate, lactic acid, vegetable gum and coloring for cheese. A process alright, but of what is anyone's guess.

But what about the far superior nutritional content found in eight ounces of natural cheese in comparison to that in eight ounces of pasteurized-process-CHEESE-food-spread? If you're keeping an avid eye on the budget, ounce for ounce it will cost far less than pasteurized-process-CHEESE-food any day.

Brand XXX 8 oz. jar - 49 cents.

Contents: 20% butterfat, 60% moisture
             Cheese
             Whey solids
             Sodium phosphate
             Lactic acid
             Vegetable gum
             Coloring

You're lucky if you get two ounces of real cheese.

Brand XXX 10 oz. jar - $1.15 in a stoneware crock or 69 cents in a plastic bag. (A so-called "Gourmet" spread.)

Contents: 31% butterfat, 52% moisture
             American brick cheese
             Muenster cheese
             Whey solids
             Non-fat dry milk
             Sodium phosphate
             Salt
             Lactic Acid
             Coloring

We estimate you get all of five ounces of real cheese. (Though there are many other types and brands, we won't bore you as they differ very little in price, ingredients and flavor, or lack of same.)

But does natural cheese "go" as far as a cheese spread and dips? No, of course it does not. However, if you want to extend the budget, if you are a compulsive cracker spreader, or if you are one of those people who simply must have a mix, blend, or spread on your cocktail table, by all means do. But make your own. It's far less expensive than buying it ready-blended in those cute little jars, and besides, as we said, *that's* not cheese.

ROQUEFORT CHEESE DIP

1   3-ounce package Roquefort cheese (crumbled)
½   pound cottage cheese
2   tablespoons dry sherry (substitute cognac or other
     brandy)
1   teaspoon grated onion
2-3 dashes Tabasco sauce
Salt
Pepper
Sufficient milk to make a smooth dip

Combine cheeses, add sherry and seasoning. Beat in sufficient milk to make a smooth dip. Makes about two cups.
Cost: approximately 85 cents. Processed Roquefort cheese
food spread: 39 cents for five ounces (½ cup).

CHEDDAR CHEESE SPREAD

½   pound soft cheddar (crumbled)
½   pound cottage cheese
1   teaspoon prepared mustard
2   tablespoons chili sauce
Salt
Pepper
Sufficient milk to make a smooth spread

Cream cheddar cheese with cottage cheese. Add remaining
ingredients, using sufficient milk to make a smooth spread.
Cost: 70 cents for approximately three cups spread. Cost:
five-ounce jar (½ cup) "Gourmet" style cheddar cheese
spread, 89 cents.

"STORE" CHEESE SPREAD

(Any sharp cheese)

1	cup (¼ lb.) "store" cheese (grated)
1	6-ounce package cream cheese
1	teaspoon prepared horseradish

Dash Tabasco sauce
Salt
Pepper
Sufficient milk to make a smooth spread

Combine and blend ingredients, adding sufficient milk to make a smooth spread. Beat until light and fluffy. Cost: about 85 cents for approximately three cups spread. Cost: eight ounces (one cup) processed "store" cheese spread, 49 cents.

PINEAPPLE COTTAGE CHEESE DIP

2	cups (1 pound) cottage cheese
1	cup crushed pineapple with 2 tablespoons juice
1	teaspoon grated onion
¼	teaspoon salt

Blend cottage cheese with pineapple, pineapple juice, onion and salt until smooth. Beat until light and fluffy. Cost: 55 cents for 3½ cups. Cost: five-ounce jar (½ cup) processed pineapple cheese spread, 39 cents.

CHEESE SPREAD A LA MAISON

1½ to 2 cups	any grated or shredded leftover cheese (or combination of compatible cheeses)
2 to 3	tablespoons butter
1 to 2	tablespoons salad oil
1 to 3	tablespoons bourbon, cognac, or blended whiskey
2 to 3	dashes of Tabasco sauce (optional)

Combine ingredients and beat until smooth. Add more or less liquid depending on dryness of cheese. Refrigerate, well covered, at least two days before serving. It will keep indefinitely and improve with age. Additional cheese, bourbon, cognac or whiskey may be added as needed or desired.

HORS D'OEUVRES NOT FOR BUYING

What----? Well, frozen cheese straws for one thing. In fact, we suggest you put them at the very top of your "don't buy" list. Why? The price, that's why. There are a few people who can afford such folly, but these are the people whose cook sends the second maid out to shop, and they don't need them. In fact, if Madame should happen to find such an item while checking her monthly bill from the grocer, Madame should fire the cook as unworthy of the name.

Cheese straws are for making, and if you don't have the time, well, make something else. Frozen commercially, they

38

cost about 79 cents a dozen and up, or about three cents a bite. You can make approximately seven dozen for the same 79 cents. Just a teensy difference, what?

CHEESE STRAWS

¼	pound butter (room temperature)
1	3-ounce package cream cheese
¼	cup crumbled Roquefort cheese, packed down
2	cups flour
⅛	teaspoon cayenne pepper
½	teaspoon salt

Cream butter with cheeses. Blend in flour and seasoning, form into a ball. Chill several hours or over night. Form dough into a log and cut into thin slices or roll out on a lightly floured board. Cut into strips or any shape desired. Bake on a lightly floured cookie sheet in a preheated 400° F. oven for eight to ten minutes or until lightly browned.

Makes about 60 cheese rounds or 80 straws.

Cost: about 80 cents or one cent a straw.

You may substitute one cup (packed down) sharp cheddar cheese instead of the cream and Roquefort cheeses, or you may use any combination of cheeses in your refrigerator. The seasoning is also up to you; garlic salt is great if your crowd likes garlic. So are a few caraway seeds.

Note: Just like "commercial," you can freeze your baked cheese straws. Simply place them on a cookie sheet in freezer until firm, then wrap in neat packages and store in freezer.

39

When guests drop in simply open a package, place straws on a cookie sheet or foil, and "bake" for about five minutes (or until hot) in a preheated 350°F. oven.

Don't have time? Make instead:

QUICK CHEESE HORS D'OEUVRES

Cut the crust from sliced white or wholewheat bread. How many slices? How much bread do you have on hand, How many people are coming, or how hungry do you think they will be? No matter how many slices, roll each slice flat with a rolling pin, spread each with butter, sprinkle with grated cheese and roll up jelly roll fashion, and press edges together. Slice each roll in half. Place on foil or flat tray in single layer, not touching, and place in freezer until firm. Store frozen in plastic bags or wrapped in foil until ready to bake. Bake at 350°F. until lightly browned.

P.S. You don't have to freeze them, but for some reason they taste better, lighter and more puffy, when you do.

P.S. Again - You can spread flattened bread with any (home-made, we do hope) cheese spread, deviled ham or meat paste. Freeze and bake in the same way.

Note: This goes for all those expensive little boxes of frozen hors d'oeuvres. Make your own, or don't as you prefer, but do not buy frozen "ready made." Bachelors sans house boy: take the girl out. Career girls: you'll be more apt to impress a male guest by putting your money in the best liquor you can afford. Let the "go withs" be anything you have the time and patience to make.

What else? Well, crackers for a second "don't buy" go high on our list. Those "buttery," salty, "ritzy" kind, cheese flavored kind, chicken flavored kind, sesame, onion, and bacon flavored kind. In fact, any kind.

Sacre Dieu! What a sacrilege! We can very clearly hear you protesting. "Why, they are a part of the good American way of life, abundance at only 49 cents for the jumbo size box, and good with everything from peanut butter to caviar, too."

Really dear girl, who says? The firm who makes them, no doubt. But if you agree, it is only because you have been sold, once again, on a product that is not good for you, unnecessary and does not, no really does not, enhance any food with which it is served or spread.

To put your health first: these crackers (the flavors vary, but the basic ingredients remain much the same) supply only empty calories. They contain no appreciable nutrition, they can contribute only to overweight.

Forty nine cents is not a large sum, but it is too much for something you do not need and are better off without.

As to flavor, they overpower the subtle taste of good cheese, make labor lost of even the simplest of patés, and what they do to caviar! Well, all we can say is what a waste, what a waste!

Give them to the children? For shame. You, my friend, are lazy or don't know what you are about. These little round wafers of homogenized shortening, flour and artificial flavor are stomach fillers, no more, no less. Pacifiers to be sure. But they destroy the child's appetite for other foods that *are* advantageous to both growth and good health.

Crackers for good cheeses, patés, spreads and dips

41

should be unsalted, or only lightly salted. They should be bland so that they do not overpower or destroy the particular food they are served under or with.

If you are a weight watcher, eliminate them entirely. Let your "go with" be instead, crisp thin slices of raw turnips, carrot ovals cut Oriental style at a forty five degree angle, or celery hearts the freshest and best you can buy.

If you must have something flour based, let it be melba toast - and make it at home from day-old French bread that you would have otherwise thrown out. Waste not, have the best and save your 49 cents; it will buy you at least one small bunch of spring flowers. One does not live by crackers alone, at least not yet, or so we fervently hope.

FRENCH MELBA TOAST

Simple, really. Just put thin slices of French bread in a very low oven (about 150°F.) until crisp and dry.

RECIPES TO EAT OUT BY

Swiss Cheese Fondue, with Kirsch Ersatz
(The secret ingredient is money)

(From a current cookbook on quick and easy French cooking, American convenience food style.)

You will need: one package of refrigerator fondue mix, one ounce Kirsch, one truffle (one truffle?), one small loaf of frozen "heat and brown" French type bread, a double boiler, a mixing spoon, two individual earthenware casseroles, two forks, two small plates, a large knife, and about 30 minutes. Cost: approximately $2.85, serves two.
And this is only the appetizer. Shall we dine out, perhaps at Le Pavillon?   Or serve instead:

GRUYERE "NATURAL"
WITH BLACK JUMBO OLIVES

You will need: ¼ pound natural Gruyere cheese, about one dozen jumbo size black olives, one knife, one plate and a small bowl.

You will cut the cheese into bite size cubes. Place it on an attractive small serving plate. Drain and place the olives in a bowl. You will then serve them "au natural" (you pick them up with your fingers).

Cost: about 70 cents, more than enough for two servings.

Note: You can save leftovers and bonus: there are no sticky pans, plates, and forks to wash up, a perfect example (ask any Frenchman) of instant haute cuisine.

The young woman who wrote the charming little cookbook from which we swiped the preceding fondue recipe tells us, in a charming little introduction, that the idea for substituting "already prepared," "packaged," canned and mixed foods for slow cooking French food came to her while attending the famous Cordon Bleu School for Haute Cuisine in Paris. It seemed, she thought while watching a particularly intricate dish being prepared, absolutely pointless to waste so many hours in a kitchen making basic sauces and stocks, and flash! Like a light it came to her. Why not simply use canned soup instead! Wow! What an idea! After all, she reasoned with perfect American logic, if you dress up a dish to look French, you know, add truffles and garni and stuff, very few people back home would ever know the difference. Of course she was right. Oh, how right she was!

However, we digress. The subject is fondue, not sauces or soup, but it did come to us like a flash while reading this recipe that this was *one* lesson our girl must have missed. Because, it saves no time at all to make fondue from "packaged-prepared." Swiss fondue is simply cheese melted with white wine plus a little flour for thickening, and you can make a gallon of the stuff for the price of a mix. In addition, unless your aim is simply to impress everybody with how filthy rich you are, truffles are not needed. They are frightfully expensive little things and their delicate flavor would be lost in this dish.

Note: She must have missed this lesson because no French chef, haute or otherwise, would suggest fondue as an appetizer. Fondue in France, as in every civilized country, is served only as a late supper dish. Make it, however, whenever you want to, for breakfast even, though the good Lord help you through the day. However do make it the only way it can be made and still be rightfully called fondue.

FONDUE

½   pound Swiss cheese*
1   teaspoon flour
1   quart any good dry white wine*
¼   cup kirsch*
    French bread

Grate cheese and sprinkle with flour. Pour wine into fondue pot. Place over medium flame until steamy hot. Add cheese, a little at a time, stirring after each addition until melted. Add kirsch and you have it, fondue as made by the Swiss.

To eat it, each person spears a cube of crusty French bread with his own fondue fork, dips it into the fondue, twirls it around, then without dribbling more than he can help onto the table, pops it into his mouth.

It's to be eaten between sips of wine.

Serves two to four.

* The Swiss take their measurements a little more casually - but you can't get by with being casual in an American cookbook. No American proofreader would allow it. But between you and me, fondue is simply a matter of adding grated cheese to hot wine until you have a mixture thick enough to stick to the cubes of bread.

SOUPS TO TAKE
AND
SOUPS TO MAKE

SOUPS TO TAKE
AND SOUPS TO MAKE

Take two cans of chicken soup, the condensed variety. Put them 'way back in an inconspicuous spot on your kitchen shelf.

When that nasty, bitchy little bitch of a girl at the office (the one who flirted with that man in your life) is home sick in bed with a bad cold, open the cans, pour them into a pretty jar or pot and take them to her.

Now -

Take the wings, gizzards and neck of three or four chickens from your freezer, or freezing compartment of your refrigerator. You will have saved them, smart girl, from the three or four broilers you broiled, or chicken (any size or variety) you cooked. No, they will not have "gone bad." You will have put them in a neat plastic bag within the last six or eight weeks.

Place them in a big pot, add a veal knuckle (that is, if your butcher will give you one — tell him it's for the dog).

If you can't get it, don't worry. Add a veal bone of any kind or the carcass of last Sunday's baked chicken, if you have it on hand. If not, proceed without; it won't make that much difference. Cover with five quarts of water, bring to a boil, let simmer gently for about 30 minutes.

Remove the scum with a big spoon as it rises to the surface. When it's clear, add two scraped carrots, a large peeled onion stuck with two cloves, two stalks of celery (tops too), a clove of garlic, a bay leaf and a few peppercorns. Simmer very gently for three to four hours. Taste, add salt. Taste again, O.K.? Strain it into a second pot. Cover and place in the refrigerator. Forget it until tomorrow. Now take it from the refrigerator and remove the congealed fat from the surface. Do you know what you have? About 12 cups of very good, clear chicken soup.

Cost: approximately 20 cents.

Cost of condensed chicken soup per can - eighteen to twenty cents. Yield per can - 1¼ cups without the water added, which is about the same strength as your homemade soup. You can add water to homemade too. I don't. I like the flavor of rich soup, not water. But it's a matter of taste.

What can you do with this much soup? You can heat and eat "as is" or you can store it in your refrigerator (up to one week - after that reheat to boiling and refrigerate again) to use as needed in any recipe from the ladies' magazines that start with "Take two cans of chicken soup or stock!"

You can freeze it too. One easy way, pour into freezer tray. Freeze until firm, remove from tray in neat little blocks. Place in plastic bag, store in freezer.

Oh yes, you can heat some and add cooked rice and vegetables and maybe some diced cooked chicken (left over from last night's dinner). You can serve some sandwiches and well, mmmmmmmm, hot soup for lunch!

If you don't like chicken soup, you can take her canned beef broth, which can also be made at home for less money than "boughten." The big difference though, is that the flavor is unlike anything found in a can, satisfying, health-giving, rib sticking, meaty and rich.

Take about two pounds beef bones with some meat still clinging to them and two pounds veal bones (saved from last Sunday's veal chops and Sunday's before that roast beef, or bought from your butcher (still very inexpensive). Put them in a roasting pan and partially cover with onion slices (one large peeled Bermuda onion will do nicely). Place in a hot (400° F.) oven for about 30 minutes, or until onion and bones are nicely browned. Transfer to a large soup kettle and cover with five quarts of water. Pour a little water into the roasting pan, bring to a boil on top of the stove, scrape up all the browned bits and pieces that have clung to the sides and bottom of the pan, then pour this into the soup kettle too.

Now add a scraped carrot or two, one or two peeled onions, a few sprigs of parsley, a bay leaf and the green leafy tops from a bunch of celery, a teaspoon of salt, a few peppercorns and if you have it and want to, any left-over cooked or raw beef in your refrigerator. Turn heat low and leave the kitchen for other pleasures or work (which depends on you and how you look at things), and let it simmer gently away for about three hours. Remove from heat, let cool, strain into containers, refrigerate. Makes about three quarts. Remove and discard congealed fat from surface before reheating or cool, strain, refrigerate until fat may be removed in solid block, pour into one-quart containers and freeze. Or freeze in ice cube trays, store in plastic bags in freezer as per instructions for chicken soup if it suits your convenience. It should, it's such an easy way to use just the amount you want - no less, no more.

Cost: If you saved the bones, only about 15 cents. If not, bargain with your butcher, it can't cost more than a few cents additional.

When you have these two basic soups in your refrigerator, you are well on your way to honest-to-goodness real, not ersatz, gourmet food. They are the beginnings of many, many great but quick-making soups, sauces, stews and casserole dishes. For example:

ONION SOUP

Melt two tablespoons butter in a saucepan, add two large peeled, thinly sliced onions. We prefer the purple kind, but don't let us sway you, any large mild onion will do. Cook, stirring until soft but not browned. Add one teaspoon flour. Stir a minute longer. Add one quart (4 cups) beef

stock. Simmer gently for about 10 minutes and correct seasoning with salt and pepper. You can serve it with or without croutons and a sprinkling of parmesan cheese, or pour it into individual oven proof casseroles, float a slice of French bread on each, sprinkle with grated parmesan cheese, and place under a broiler flame until cheese is melted and lightly browned.

Cost: about 16 cents.

CREAM OF CHICKEN SOUP

Melt a tablespoon of butter in a sauce pan, stir in one teaspoon flour. Cook until bubbly. Add one quart (4 cups) clear chicken soup. Stir until smooth. Simmer gently for 15 to 20 minutes. Mix one egg yolk with two or three tablespoons cream and a little of the hot soup, stir into hot soup, bring almost to boil. Correct seasoning with salt, add ¼ cup diced chicken and serve. (Serves three to four as a main course, six for a first course.)

Sounds rich and expensive? Well, rich it is, but expensive it is not. Cost: about 36 cents (and that's with real cream).

VICHYSSOISE

Heat one tablespoon butter in a large saucepan, add two chopped scallions. Saute until soft but not browned (two to three minutes). Add two peeled and chopped potatoes and two cups clear chicken soup, ½ teaspoon salt, ¼ teaspoon white pepper; cover and simmer gently for 30 minutes. Puree in a blender or force through a sieve. Return to heat.

Add one cup milk. Cook for two or three minutes. Stir in a second cup milk. Refrigerate until well chilled. Serve sprinkled with chopped chives.

Cost: 25 cents.

All soup recipes serve four to six generously.

SOUP NOT FOR BUYING
CANNED, TO SUBSTITUTE FOR SAUCE:

Repeat after me, friend, canned soup is not sauce. No, thick, creamed, clear, condensed, frozen, tomato, potato, onion, green pea, cheddar cheese, or oyster, gumbo, bisque, or "stew," canned soup is not, nor ever will be, sauce. Not even when you add a dashing tablespoon of sherry. It is soup. It's sometimes thick like sauce. It "binds together" other ingredients like sauce. It even looks like sauce. But sauce it is not.

What's in the pretty cans? Canned soup, that's what. Are we "cooking young" when we substitute soup for sauce? No, sweetie, we are just cooking bad, and expensive.

But we do save time (put that word as befits its importance in two color neon blinking lights) when we use it as a cooking ingredient when making, say poulet au vin? Yes, we do, just a bit, indeedy we do. But we would save ourselves even more if we didn't bother at all, because we would not be making poulet au vin. We would be making chicken stewed in canned soup, and this is not worth the effort. Americans, this is not nice. This does not taste good. Better, when kitchen speed is of the essence, that we be honest, render unto Escoffier that which is Escoffier's and just broil the chicken and heat up the soup.

Canned soup, dear reader, does not enhance any dish, nor is it needed. What's more, each time you substitute a simple white sauce for creamed canned soup you will save 5 to 35 cents, and when you use your own homemade chicken, fish or beef stock, or simply water plus perhaps a veal bone, a few vegetables and seasoning, you will save even more. Besides this, your chicken, fish, meat, pasta or what have you will taste like chicken, fish, meat, pasta or what have you, not commercially made, bland and insipid, but unmistakable canned soup.

If you want more of a bead drawn on this, if you don't know or have forgotten, each time you read a new recipe that calls for this modern "time saving" ingredient, look up and compare it to an old-fashioned version of the same dish. It may or may not take longer to cook, but usually you will find that it requires very little additional effort to make, and seven out of ten times, the cost will be less.

When a "new" short cut canned recipe calls for creamed soup plus ¼ to ½ cup milk as an ingredient, use instead 1½ cups of milk and thicken dish by adding one tablespoon of butter creamed with one teaspoon flour, stirring until smooth, and add seasoning to your taste. Substitute ¼ to ½ cup white wine, or chicken, beef or fish stock, for an equivalent of milk if desired; and add a dash of sherry if you really do like the stuff.

Or, make sauce first and add other ingredients to same pan: melt two tablespoons butter in sauce pan, stir in one tablespoon flour. When bubbly, slowly add 1½ cups milk, stir until smooth and slightly thickened. There you are, a basic white sauce (no mixes or cans needed). Add seasoning plus whatever ingredients you desire. Cook over low heat, stirring often until added ingredients are cooked or hot.

This amount of sauce is equivalent to one can of creamed soup plus ¼ to ½ cup milk (the usual proportions for soups, canned, creamed, masquerading as sauce).

CHEDDAR CHEESE SAUCE

Stir ¼ cup crumbled or shredded cheddar cheese into basic white sauce.

Cost: about 27 cents.

Cost of frozen cheddar cheese soup as sauce: 39 cents with milk added (1½ cups).

CREAM OF MUSHROOM SAUCE

Add two finely chopped fresh mushrooms to butter in basic sauce recipe. Cook stirring one minute before adding flour. Continue as per instructions.

Cost: about 30 cents.

Cost of mushroom soup as sauce: about 32 cents (with 1½ cups of milk added).

CREAM OF CELERY SAUCE

Add two tablespoons finely chopped celery to butter in basic cream sauce recipe. Proceed as directed in making mushroom sauce.

Cost: about 25 cents.

Cost of celery soup as sauce: about 31 cents (with 1½ cups milk added).

CREAM OF SHRIMP SAUCE

Add two large chopped fresh cooked shrimp to butter in basic cream sauce recipe. Proceed as directed in mushroom sauce. Substitute ½ to one cup water in which shrimp was cooked for an equivalent amount of milk.

Cost: about 31 cents.

Cost of frozen shrimp bisque used as sauce: about 59 cents (with 1½ cups milk added).

CREAM OF TOMATO SAUCE

Make basic cream sauce as directed. Stir in two tablespoons tomato puree.

Cost: about 22 cents.

Cost of cream of tomato soup as sauce: about 21 cents (with 1½ cups milk added).

When new style recipes call for one can of cold creamed soup to be combined with other ingredients for baked dishes, simply sprinkle layers of food lightly with flour in baking dish. Dot each layer with butter, then pour 1½ cups milk over surface. If desired, substitute ¼ to ½ cup fish, chicken or meat stock depending on type of dish, for an equal amount of milk--and you should desire. It will enhance the finished product.

SAUCE ESPAGNOLE

(French brown sauce, the base from which most dark sauces of France are derived, to substitute for non-creamy type canned soup when used as an ingredient or as "sauce.")

It is sad but true that the French food snob, very much like the French wine snob who depopularizes French wine by his snobbism, has done more to discourage good French food in this country than he has to forward this civilized pleasure. Though certainly haute cuisine (another subject, really) is an art that requires time, effort, knowledge, and skill, too many would-be gourmets make entirely too much of what is relatively simple: home-style French cooking. The good French cook (and let's face it, she is, after all, the best cook in the world) actually spends less effort and time in her kitchen than does the mix and match, heat and eat, brown and serve American non-cooking master. Naturelment, she also spends a great deal less money.

French sauces are a perfect example. In that country, the best of those dishes called menagere, "family style," are almost always based on a sauce made from slow cooking stock of bones, a few pennies worth of vegetables, herbs, seasoning. Slowly simmered, these sauces take no effort and very little actual work. They need only occasional watching. Made ahead, they are cooled, stored, and used as needed in any number and variety of quick cooking dishes that taste as though they had been cooking for hours.

Certainly it is far easier and quicker to get a meal to the table when half the work has already been done. With a basic brown sauce in your refrigerator (it may be stored frozen for weeks), an honest, inexpensive and extremely nutritious French meal takes no more time to prepare than any other, including those soup based, one dish, casserole suppers so dear to the hearts of ladies' page food editors.

SAUCE ESPAGNOLE
(Brown Sauce)

1	large chopped onion
1	small scraped and finely chopped carrot
2	tablespoons oil
2	tablespoons butter
2	tablespoons flour
6	cups clear beef stock (see beef soup recipe)

1   sprig parsley
1   bay leaf
1   clove garlic (optional)
2   tablespoons tomato puree

Sauté onion and carrot in oil and butter in deep, heavy sauce pan until onion is transparent. Add flour and cook, stirring until flour, onion and carrot are lightly browned. Add three cups beef stock and cook, stirring until mixture thickens. Add remaining stock, parsley, bay leaf, and garlic. Simmer gently for about two hours or until sauce has reduced by half. Stir in tomato puree. Strain into containers. Seal container with foil. Refrigerate up to one week. Use as needed, or cool sauce, pour into ice cube trays and freeze until firm. Remove from trays and store in well-sealed plastic bag in freezer for two to three months. Eight cubes make one cup sauce.

How to use? Substitute 1 cup brown sauce and ½ cup water or 1 cup brown sauce and ½ cup dry wine for one can condensed beef, or chicken, stock or onion soup, Creole gumbo, Scotch broth, etc. in any canned soup based recipe.

Use to make sauce for cooked meats, chicken, or game.

Use in French recipe calling for brown sauce, or add one cup water to one cup sauce and use in any recipe in place of beef or chicken stock.

SHERRY SAUCE

Cook one cup of brown sauce over low flame until reduced to half. Add ¼ cup dry sherry. Season to taste with salt and pepper. Serve with beef, chicken, or veal.

SAUCE BORDELAISE

Cook two finely chopped scallions or shallots in ½ cup dry red wine until wine is reduced to half. Add one cup brown sauce. Simmer gently until again reduced to half. Season to taste with salt and pepper. Serve with any cooked meat.

SAUCE ROMAINE

Cook one tablespoon sugar over low flame in heavy sauce-pan until it turns light golden. Add ¼ cup white wine vine-gar. Cook, stirring until vinegar has almost evaporated. Add one cup brown sauce. Bring to boil. Add ¼ cup raisins. Simmer five minutes. Serve with duck, ham or pork.

All sauces are for approximately four servings.

There are as many recipes for poulet au vin as there are ways to use brown sauce. Here is a classic example of how to do both.

POULET AU VIN

1	2 pound chicken cut into serving pieces
2	tablespoons butter
1	tablespoon oil
2	tablespoons brandy
½	cup dry white wine
1	cup brown sauce

Brown chicken pieces in oil and butter. Pour off excess cooking fat from pan. Turn up heat. Add brandy, ignite, let flame burn out. Add wine and brown sauce. Cover, simmer until chicken is tender. Makes four to six servings.

BEEF WITH GREEN PEPPERS

¼   cup oil
1   pound top round (cut across grain in very thin strips)
½   cup water
½   teaspoon salt
1   large purple (Italian) onion cut into thin slices
2   green peppers (seeded and cut into 2 inch strips)
1   small clove garlic (optional)
1   cup brown sauce
1   teaspoon cornstarch mixed to a paste with one teaspoon soy sauce and one tablespoon water.

Heat oil in heavy skillet. Brown beef strips, add water and let simmer 30 minutes. Then add remaining ingredients except cornstarch mixture. Cover, simmer ten minutes or until green pepper is crisp and tender. Stir in cornstarch mixture. Serve over white rice.

TV DINNERS

TV DINNERS

Take four TV dinners, four cola drinks, one package "heat and eat" rolls, one frozen apple pie, and one pint of "Ready Pack" ice cream.

Please, you take them, the thought makes me sick. What to do with them? First, heat the TV dinners. Now smile and say just like that lady in the magazine advertisement "Come and get it gang," but don't for God's sake, serve it to your family. Throw it to the dogs. The dogs won't say "Yummie" like the cute little girl in the advertisement, but they will enjoy it. Well, maybe.

Next open the cola drinks and pour them on your pot plants. I knew a man who grew the most gorgeous philodendron that way; he said it was the sugar that did it.

The frozen pie, ice cream, and "heat and eat" rolls, well now, here's a constructive thought for owners of upright freezers. Wrap them in foil (so no one can possibly know what's in there) and place them at the very bottom. Makes everything else so much easier to get to.

Now that's taken care of, let's prepare an authentic French peasant dinner.

Braised Beef with Vegetables

French Bread

Red Wine

Camembert Cheese

Crisp Apple Slices

Lace Cookies

Coffee

All you really have to make is the braised beef with vegetables. Buy the camembert cheese and the red wine from a good cheese and wine shop, respectively. No supermarket for these items please. Buy them with care. Make sure the cheese is ripe and the wine an honest one. (Good, not fine, Italian, American and even French wine can be had for a modest price.) If you are not sure of your judgment on these items, rely on trusted and knowledgeable merchants who know their products. Yes, there are a few around, and they are worth seeking out.

Buy two of the best apples you can find; one half per serving is ample. If not in season or the price is prohibitive, substitute fresh peaches, pears or small bunches of grapes. All still too high? Serve each person a handful of raisins instead. Nice with the cheese and great with that last sip of wine. The cookies you will have made one leisurely hour "some time ago." (See cookie recipe page 125.)

Bon appetit.

Just for the record, before you begin, here's a breakdown of the difference between an honest French meal and TV commercials plus America's favorite (?) drink and dessert.

TV DINNER

4	TV dinners, 69 cents each	$2.76
1	Frozen apple pie	.55
4	Cola drinks	.40
1	Pint ice cream	.69
	Instant coffee	.05
8	"Heat and Eat" rolls	.59
		$5.04

French Dinner

Braised beef with vegetables for 4	$2.60
Loaf French bread	.30
Wine to go into and with meal	2.00
Camembert cheese (4 small portions)	.90
Apples, 2 large	.30
Homemade lace cookies, 3 per person	.05
Coffee	.10
	$6.25

Well, what do you know. We spend all of $1.21 cents more and all that work besides. Oh well, could we talk about flavor and nutrition perhaps? Or maybe the advantages of honest food well prepared? No, not really, it has to be experienced. May we suggest you try.

BRAISED BEEF WITH VEGETABLES

Cut one pound lean stew meat (beef chuck) into 2" cubes. Brown them in two tablespoons of oil in a heavy skillet (one with a tight fitting lid) over medium flame. Use a long handled spoon and keep stirring meat so it is evenly seared on all sides. When lightly browned, sprinkle ½ teaspoon sugar over meat. Continue stirring until meat is quite dark. Light three tablespoons brandy (blended whiskey substitutes nicely) in a soup ladle. Pour flaming over meat. Let flame burn out, remove skillet from heat. Add three to four ripe tomatoes, cut into quarters, one small chopped onion, one bay leaf, and one clove garlic (optional), plus ½ teaspoon salt and ¼ teaspoon coarse ground black pepper. Return skillet to heat. Pour in one cup red wine, one cup beef stock (see recipe, page 50). Cover, let simmer gently over low flame until meat is tender (1½ to 2 hours). Shake pan occasionally, but do not remove lid anymore than you can resist. There should be very little liquid in final dish. So unless you want "lots more gravy" do not add additional liquid. A little more wine if you must, or beef stock, but never water; it weakens the flavor. About 30 minutes before meat is tender, add eight small peeled white onions, stirring them under the meat and into the liquid. Cover, let cook 15 minutes. Uncover, add eight to ten very small carrots (stir them into the liquid as you did the onions). Cover again and cook until carrots are tender. Serve now, or refrigerate (or even freeze if you like) and reheat.

What to do with other frozen TV dinners and dishes? Gee, we have a number of excellent suggestions, but there

70

are some things one just does not put on paper - at least not in a book on food. After all, we are not Norman Mailer.

But we would suggest this: don't buy them at all. Pleasure is one of the duties of life; and well-seasoned, carefully prepared meals are one of our most civilized pleasures.

Commercially frozen dishes and dinners are, at their best, bland and insipid. They are, of necessity, under-seasoned to appeal to a mass market, and sad to relate, though they may sufficiently appease the appetite, they do not sufficiently nourish the body or make for truly pleasurably eating. Convenient? What's convenient about unnecessarily wasting your money? Good meals, nourishing meals, easy meals and even exciting gourmet meals can be cooked "for real," with no more effort and far less expense than heating and assembling a meal of mostly frozen, commercially prepared messes, or should we say more politely, dishes.

It can be proven, dish after frozen dish, but there's not enough space in our book. However, here is an excellent "for instance" to bring home a few points, taken from real life, so help us!

Career girl dilemma:

Career girl, in weak moment, five A.M. after a night on the town, asks very eligible man to "home cooked" meal. Girl can't cook, or at least has been brainwashed by expensive and complicated gourmet recipes in fashion magazines (her only reading) into believing she can't cook. Wants to impress man with elegant dinner, prove her desirability as wife to rising young executive, in kitchen as well as in parlor and bedroom.

Tall order as our girl arrives home at 5:15, must grocery shop, cook meal and look glamourous by 7:30. Decides prepared frozen food is the only answer. Chooses this menu:

Veal Stroganoff with noodles

Endive Salad - Roquefort Dressing

Buttered Parkerhouse Rolls

Red Wine

=

Chocolate Eclairs

Coffee

Home from the grocer she prepares salad, sets table and opens wine, then spends balance of time before date arrives to dress. After all, it's relatively easy, she reasoned, to prepare an "almost all prepared for you" meal. Except for the noodles, it's just heat (or thaw) and eat, or so it says on the package.

Our girl, however, has been misguided about the convenience of convenient meals. Too many trips to the kitchen made the role of unharried, unhurried, gracious hostess impossible. Veal takes longer to heat than stated on package (most makers of frozen prepared foods are over-optimistic in this matter). Noodles cannot be cooked until veal is almost ready, and frozen rolls must be watched; too long in the oven, they are dried out and crumbly (this often happens to commercially frozen breads). What's more, when meal is finally assembled, it proves a disappointment. Ten ounces of veal and sauce are not adequate for serving two hungry people as a main course. Bottled Roquefort dressing is too tart, not compatible with wine. As a result, man does not eat salad. And to complete fiasco, too much pasta and bread (and not enough meat) make for too starchy a meal. Makes both man and girl "loggy" and dull, not at best for balance of evening. Result? Unimportant really, as man proved to be a bore anyway. Evening, however, not a total loss. Girl learns lesson. Next time serves even more eligible man less convenient (much less expensive), made-ahead meal.

Beef and Zucchini Roma

with

Grated Romano Cheese

Crusty Italian Bread

Chianti

=

Oranges Oriental

=

Butter cookies

Coffee

Arrives home 5:15. Shops for groceries and wine, 5:15 to 5:30. Prepares dessert 5:35 to 5:50. Places in refrigerator to chill. Cooks beef and zucchini. Leaves on back of stove to reheat. Grates romano cheese, sets table, slices bread, takes made-ahead butter cookies from freezer*, and opens wine, now 6:30. Spends one hour glamourizing self. Ready to greet guest at 7:30. Needs only five minutes to reheat main dish.

As to the difference in price, well, sans liquid refreshment, here are the cold cash facts:

Our girl's cash outlay for convenient (?) convenience food meal:

10 oz. package gourmet type veal Stroganoff	$1.98
8 oz. package flat noodles	.35
8 oz. bottle gourmet type Roquefort dressing	.89
Fresh endive	.60
Frozen rolls	.59
Frozen eclairs	.63
	$5.04

Had on hand: salt, pepper, butter and coffee.

* See butter cookie recipe, page 128

74

Cash outlay for convenient but cooked "for real" meal:

1 pound ground chuck	$ .80
1 large tomato	.35
1 purple onion	.10
1 pound zucchini	.35
⅓ pound romano cheese	.50
Italian bread	.30
4 large seedless oranges	.40
½ pint ice cream	.35
	$3.15

Had on hand: oil, butter, salt, pepper, sugar, hot sauce, coffee, and homemade cookies.

Just for the record, the cost of six homemade butter cookies added about five cents to total cost of meal. See page 128 for recipe.

BEEF AND ZUCCHINI ROMA

Heat one tablespoon each butter and cooking oil in a large heavy skillet (one with a lid). Add one pound ground chuck and cook, stirring until meat is no longer pink (takes about two minutes over a medium flame). Now chop up one large ripe tomato and add it to meat; stir a half minute. Then add one large, peeled and chopped purple onion and three or four medium sized zucchini, sliced rather thin (about one pound zucchini), a few dashes hot sauce and generous sprinkling of freshly ground black pepper. Hold pepper grinder over skillet and just grind away. Now add salt, lightly here, love, you can always add more. Stir to blend everything nicely. Cover the pan and cook over medium heat only until zucchini is just tender. Don't overcook. If dinner is delayed, you can always reheat. It actually tastes better for waiting. Serve with freshly grated romano cheese, lots of it, and crusty Italian bread to mop up the sauce.

ORANGES ORIENTAL

Peel three large seedless oranges, taking care to remove as much "white" as possible. Slice into a large (and pretty, if you have one) serving bowl. Cover bowl and refrigerate. Next place in a saucepan: ¾ cup sugar, ½ cup water, juice of one orange and rind of ½ orange (all white removed), cut into thin, thin julienne strips. Place over medium heat and cook, stirring frequently, until sugar is dissolved. Let simmer gently until liquid is reduced to half, about 10 minutes. Remove from heat, cool, pour over oranges in serving dish, and refrigerate again until ready to serve. Top each serving with a scoop of ice cream.

TV FOOD
NOT FOR BUYING

Here's a complete spring (?) menu yet, from a national magazine whose editor should, and actually does, know better. However (and can you blame the poor thing?), advertisers must come first and then, as Mama used to say, a long time - nobody. After all, there's her job to consider, and besides it really is work dreaming up new ways to promote such products as Toasty Fruity Pop Pops and Whipped Topping Mix, month after month after month. We do think she did well (no, not for you, dear, for the advertiser) with this particular dinner for spring.

SPRING MENU

Broiled Ham Steak with Mustard Hollandaise
(Hollandaise made from Dehydrated Sauce Mix)

Asparagus
(frozen)

Country Mashed Potatoes
(Instant Potatoes and
Corn Flakes)

Spring Salad
(Canned Tomato Slices
Packed in Salad Dressing)

Strawberry-Raspberry Ice Cream Cake
(Whipped Topping Mix, Toasty Fruity
Pop Pops, Ice Cream, and Frozen Raspberries)

This is spring?? The only fresh and green food is a little lettuce to hold the canned sliced tomatoes.

The copy accompanying this menu states (and there's even a breakdown of timing) that this mostly packaged, dehydrated and frozen meal takes only thirty minutes to prepare. If you work steadily (and fast) the entire thirty minutes, it's only too true.

The first ten minutes are devoted to making the dessert, an elaborate affair which, when assembled, looks rather like a baked Alaska. But it tastes, unfortunately, rather more like embalming fluid smells. This is undoubtedly due to the Toasty Fruity Pop Pops, the big thing about them being that they can remain (unrefrigerated) on a kitchen shelf practically forever, which they certainly would on ours. Anyone forced to eat them as a steady diet would want to stop the world and get off.

A second ten minutes is given to mixing up the Hollandaise sauce mix with the mustard and water and stuff; putting the ham on to broil and starting the frozen asparagus. (The fact that the ham will be undercooked and the asparagus limp from overcooking matters not at all to the gal who wrote this copy; it *reads* well.)

The remaining time goes to making the instant mashed potatoes and combining them with corn flakes (this makes them country style?), saucing the ham and making the salad. A real breath of spring this last. Fresh lettuce and spinach leaves are carefully washed, torn into bite-size pieces, blotted dry, then murdered by the canned tomatoes in their very own salad dressing.

Bowls, pans and beaters used for mixing the mixes are thrown into the sink. The frozen raspberries are placed in hot water to thaw, and dinner, such as it is, is ready.

A sandwich eaten in the park would be more appropriate to the season.

Let's do just that, or prepare a bit more spring-like meal!

Here's one that may be assembled any spring evening within a little less hectic forty-five minutes.

Shad Roe Sauteed in Butter

With Lemon and Parsley Garni

Fresh Asparagus   Parsley New Potatoes
Hollandaise

Fresh Rhubarb Short Cake

Not to be outdone by our efficient, if insincere, magazine food editor, here's our own breakdown in timing.

First fifteen minutes, rhubarb is washed, sliced and put on stove to gently simmer. Potatoes are started. Hollandaise made (it will reheat). Asparagus is prepared for cooking and refrigerated until ready to put on the fire, ten minutes before serving. (We like them crisp tender.) Then, and here's the big difference from that paper-planned meal, we take ten minutes for station identification, so to speak. After a hard day, we feel the need for time out to tune in with an icy cold gin and tonic. Then back to the kitchen where we

saute our shad roe, reheat the Hollandaise, keep an eye on the now-cooking asparagus, drain the potatoes, toss them gently with parsley and butter, take the rhubarb from the stove, add sugar ...... let cool at room temperature. Then we enjoy our spring dinner for real.

We regret to say, how misleading, that an additional five minutes must be given after the main course to assemble dessert. But there's this compensating factor in our favor. Our menu also saves a bit of spring green and in the form of crisp bills; i.e. $$$.

Again, using said magazine as a guide, we give you the breakdown of prices.

For that packaged, frozen, and dehydrated spring meal (to serve four) you will need to buy:

1	2 pound fully cooked ham steak	$2.38
1	Hollandaise sauce mix	.59
2	packages frozen asparagus	1.18
1	package instant mashed potatoes	.39
1	can sliced tomatoes in salad dressing	.69
1	pint brick ice cream	.69
2	packages topping mix	.78
1	package flash thaw frozen raspberries	.39
1	package Toasty Fruity Pop Pops	.35

At a total cost of: **$7.44**

If you have on hand:

1	head Boston lettuce	about	.35
¼	pound fresh spinach	about	.05
1	lemon	about	.10
cornflakes milk butter salt and pepper	for instant mashed potatoes		.10

Total cost: .60

Total cost of meal will be: $8.04

For our fresh foods spring meal (to serve four) you will need to buy:

4	shad roe	about	$3.00
1	pound fresh asparagus	about	.70
3	pounds new potatoes	about	.50
1	pound fresh rhubarb	about	.45
1	small bunch fresh parsley	about	.15
½	pint French Vanilla ice cream	about	.40
At a total cost of:			$5.20

If you have on hand:

1	layer cake (frozen - see page 144 for recipes)	about	.25
2	eggs	about	.10
½	pound butter	about	.40
1	cup sugar	about	.05
2	lemons	about	.14
salt and pepper		about	.01
Total cost:			.95

Total cost of meal:	$6.15

The cost may be reduced further by substituting shad for shad roe, not quite as elegant, but much less expensive. Also, as the season progresses, the price of asparagus and rhubarb will go down. Ours were purchased at the very beginning.

Once upon a more innocent time of our life, we thought everyone knew how to sauté shad roe, boil potatoes, steam asparagus, and even stew rhubarb and assemble a rhubarb short cake. But that was before "nonfood" cooking. So, for the benefit of those who have been too busy "reading the directions on the package," here's the how for these simplest of all gourmet dishes.

SAUTÉED SHAD ROE

⅛   pound butter (½ stick)
4   shad roe
Salt and pepper to taste

Melt butter in skillet (one with a lid). Add shad roe. Cover and cook over medium to low heat 15 to 20 minutes, being careful not to allow the butter to brown. Remove roe to serving plates. Pour pan butter over them, sprinkle with salt and pepper. Garnish with lemon wedges and parsley sprigs. Serve at once.

PARSLEY NEW POTATOES

Scrub potatoes under cold running water. Cook over medium heat in water to cover until tender. Drain. Peel a wide strip of skin from each potato, return to same pan in which they were boiled. Add about ½ teaspoon each butter and chopped parsley for each potato. Stir gently over low heat until potatoes are well coated and piping hot. Serve at once.

ASPARAGUS

Cut off the tough ends from the stalks and use a pan designed for cooking this vegetable, if you have one. If not, place them in the bottom of a large skillet and add water to half cover them. Place tender stalks on top, out of water. Cover pan and cook over medium heat until stalks are tender. Remove and hold tips under cold running water for a few seconds. This prevents their continuing to cook. Serve plain, with melted butter, or with sauce: Hollandaise, vinaigrette, white, etc.

HOLLANDAISE SAUCE

½   cup butter (1 stick)
2   egg yolks
juice from ½ lemon

Place half the butter in a small saucepan with egg yolks and lemon juice. Place saucepan in second pan of hot water over very low heat (do not allow water to boil). Stir constantly until butter is melted. Add remaining butter and stir until sauce is thick. Serve at once, or cover and set aside. Reheat in pan of hot water, stirring constantly until ready to serve. If sauce curdles or separates at any point, beat in one tablespoon cream, stir until again smooth. Makes ¾ cup.

FRESH RHUBARB SHORT CAKE

1   pound rhubarb
4   tablespoons water
    chopped rind from ½ lemon
¾   cup sugar
4   slices plain butter, pound, or sponge cake
½   pint vanilla ice cream

Cut rhubarb into 1″ pieces. Place in saucepan, add water and lemon rind. Cover, cook over very low heat 15 to 20 minutes. Stir in sugar. Remove from heat and allow to cool. Spoon still warm rhubarb and sauce over slices of cake in small serving bowls. Top each with a scoop of ice cream and serve.

RECIPES TO EAT OUT BY

Veal Rolls "Advertiserpayoff"
(From a nationally distributed magazine dedicated to gracious living, good food, and --- canned soup)

You will need: bacon, herb seasoned stuffing mix, butter, veal, frozen broccoli spears, chicken flavored gravy base, water, frozen condensed shrimp soup, and milk (a lovely combination), shrimp, bacon, bacon grease, milk, veal and chicken. You fry the bacon, combine with part of the mix and add butter. Pound the veal and then stuff with the grease, bread crumb and butter mixture. Tie it up with string, and brown in more bacon grease. Transfer to baking dish, add frozen broccoli, and pour over the water mixed with the chicken base gravy mix. Bake for one hour; some people like their broccoli cooked for this amount of time. While it's baking, you will have time to wash that sink full of dishes. Then you heat the frozen soup with the milk, and pour it over the whole mess--we mean the broccoli and veal. You'll spend about two hours in the kitchen, but my goodness, what difference will that make? Unless you're in a hurry. Then, you could eat out, an Italian restaurant perhaps, or there is this alternative: take the same veal and make Veal Piccante, serve with crisp cooked plain broccoli, and round out the meal with boiled, imported from Italy, pasta sprinkled with freshly grated Parmesan cheese. It will take about 15 minutes to prepare, including time to open the Chianti.

VEAL PICCANTE

1   pound veal scallops
¼   cup flour
1   teaspoon salt
½   teaspoon freshly ground black pepper
2   tablespoons olive oil
2   tablespoons butter
2   tablespoons lemon juice
6   large fresh mushrooms (thinly sliced)
¼   cup dry white wine
2   tablespoons minced parsley

Have your butcher pound the veal very thin. Dip each slice in mixture of flour, salt and pepper. In a pan heat oil and butter, then add veal slices in single layer, and brown on both sides. When browned, pour off fat, add lemon juice, mushrooms and white wine. Cover and cook one minute. Remove veal to serving platter. Add parsley to pan juices, stir a few seconds only, pour over veal and enjoy. Serves four.

Price of veal rolls: about $3.50
Price of Veal Piccante: about $3.10

CHICKEN NOT FOR YOU

In pies frozen that is.

My goodness, why not? They are the perfect answer, or so they* say, when one is busy, busy, busy, and there's no time to fix lunch, or when one is a working one (or two) who comes home from "le job" simply too, too tired to cook or even eat out.

They are the perfect answer for what - a meal that's about 90% starch? About 50 cents worth of empty calories? The easy way to get fat? To be even more tired tomorrow and the day after that?

Sweetie, this is not a book on nutrition, but let me fill you in on a few, but basic, nutritional facts.

If you want to stay healthy, you must have from 60 to 70 grams of protein every day of your life,** and if you want to maintain your looks and your "youthful" vigor, you need quite a bit more than that.***

In today's modern diet, most of our protein is derived from meat, fish, fowl, egg, milk and cheese. If you do not

---

* "They" are usually those smart little people with big salaries who write that yummy copy in all those mouth watering advertisements.

** Figures based on recommendations of the Food and Nutrition Board of the National Research Council.

*** The Council has attempted to set up practical standards for the entire population, including the many families who must live on below average incomes. Most nutritionists maintain that this figure is far too low for optimal health.

get enough of these protein foods daily (or sufficient pro-
teins in other less appetizing, more fattening foods such as
soybean flour, powdered brewer's yeast, nuts and wheat
germ), the results will be poor health, saggy muscles, wrinkles,
that "can't take it" feeling, and old age long before those
retirement checks start to roll in.

So what's wrong with a frozen chicken pie supper when
you had eggs for breakfast, meat and even milk for lunch?
Only this, dear friend, only this: you don't know your pro-
teins if you think this will do the job, or you didn't count
right. Better start over and try once again.

Main sources of complete protein	Amount	Grams of Protein
Meat, fish, fowl		
boned, with little fat	¼ lb.	18 - 22
with moderate fat	¼ lb.	15 - 18
with much fat and bone	¼ lb.	10 - 15
Eggs	1	6
Whole milk, skim milk,		
butter milk	1 qt.	32 - 35
Cottage cheese	½ cup	20
American or Swiss Cheese	2 slices	10 - 12
Wheat germ	½ cup	24
Soybean flour	1 cup	60
Powdered brewer's yeast	½ cup	50
Nuts	½ cup	14 - 22

You throw away your hard earned money if the food you buy is not as good for you as it tastes good. When you buy a five-ounce frozen chicken pie, what with a bottom crust, top crust, onions, carrots, peas, sauce, and sometimes even potatoes, you're lucky, darn lucky, if you get two ounces of chicken for your 49 to 89 cents.

For about 35 cents, you can buy ¼ pound best quality chuck (20 to 22 grams of protein) and how much trouble does it really take to broil two hamburger patties, toast two buns, and slice up a tomato for salad.

Or, roast ¼ of a chicken, about 50 cents (18 to 20 grams of protein). Buy a two pound whole chicken, cut into fourths, freeze what you don't use. Wrap each fourth loosely in foil, season with salt and pepper, add a few drops water or lemon juice and dot with butter. Seal foil and bake at 350° F. until tender. It takes no longer than heating that frozen chicken pie.

Or, bake ½ pound haddock fillets, about 75 cents (19 to 22 grams of protein). Place them in a baking dish (or a foil throw away pan, even), dot with butter, add a few mild onion slices, season with salt and pepper. Cover with milk or half milk, half white wine. Bake at 350° F. for about 15 minutes. It's quicker than frozen pie yet.

However, if you live alone, eat alone, work hard and even this amount of cooking seems "for just you," too, too depressing, then for heaven's sake, don't! Two nights of each week, ask someone over to share a home-cooked meal (makes it worth the trouble). One night eat leftovers, maybe cold roast beef and a fresh baked potato. (It can't depress you to just stick a potato into an oven, can it?) Three nights eat out, and on that last night after an especially hard day, stop off at a good delicatessen and pick up ¼ pound assorted cold cuts and cheese (about 20 grams of protein), some fresh fruit, French bread, and a bottle of really good red wine. Go home, put on something comfortable, and make the evening count with the best of food and nutrition, plus the simple pleasure of serene contemplation or whatever suits your mood. Hard working, all alone, you deserve more than frozen chicken pie and poor health.

POTATOES
AND
VEGETABLES

POTATOES AND VEGETABLES

Find an old-fashioned grocer, difficult but worth it (so picturesque you know), one who sells his vegetables by weight, to your preference, rather than in neat, prewrapped packages of not enough or too much.

Ask him to weigh a 27 cent package of frozen French fries against 27 cents worth of his best Idaho potatoes.

Take the most weight for your money home. The fact that you will have to carry three pounds of raw potatoes instead of one little seven ounce box is lamentable but, after all, not really important if what you want are crisp fried potatoes without the bother of heating a large pot of oil.

Though you may have been buying cooked potatoes if you had chosen the frozen, crisp they would not have been, nor would they even slightly resemble home fries; that is, not unless you refry them. Makers of frozen French fries suggest, "for best results," you do just this. It's what they call "the preferred method."

It's far easier and much more like the real thing to use your raw potatoes and a "convenience" method called:

BROILED / FRIED POTATOES

Scrub potatoes clean under cold running water. Come now, that's not work; it takes about 15 seconds or less per potato. Do not peel, simply slice into neat ¼″ thick rounds (no need to measure, just judge by eye). Arrange them in a single layer on a long sheet of foil. Dribble a little vegetable oil directly from the bottle on each slice. Place in a 400° F. oven and bake, turning once just like frozen, except, gad, such work! You should again add oil after turning. However, in about ten minutes they will be crisp and lightly browned on the outside, mealy and delicious within. Just salt lightly and serve.

Incidentally, you can accomplish this gastronomic feat while broiling small steaks. Add halved tomatoes, sprinkled with sugar and salt, dotted with butter to the broiler and there you have it, a gourmet TV dinner, so to speak.

P.S. You can do the same thing with sweet potatoes if you are broiling a ham steak.

VEGETABLES
NOT FOR BUYING

Any frozen vegetable in butter sauce.

But they come in those neat little cook in the bag bags!!

We know that, but before you become carried away by yet another ingenious modern American miracle of packaging, may we point out: a 10 ounce package of frozen vegetables in butter sauce costs from seven to 12 cents over the price of a 10 ounce package of plain frozen vegetables. The butter sauce is simply butter plus seasoning. You can add your own for three to five cents. As to the advantage of those plastic bags, unless you plan on cooking your entire meal by this method, serving it on paper plates, and eating it with throw away knives and forks, there is none.

To cook plain frozen vegetables with butter and seasoning, you get out a pan, add the vegetables and water and salt. Cook them, drain, add butter plus seasoning, and serve, right? Then you put the pan aside and when dinner is done, you wash it along with your other dishes and wipe it dry and put it away. Right again.

To cook frozen vegetables in a plastic bag, you do very much the same thing but with this slight difference. Get out the pan, add water, bring to boil, add bag of vegetables. Cook the required time, remove bag, open it (a tricky little job in itself), and serve. Then you put the pan aside and when dinner is done, you wipe it dry and put it away.

How much time does it take to wash that one extra pan along with your other dishes? About 20 seconds might be a good guess. Obviously, unless you have no other dishes to wash, the work saved is nil. And there's this disadvantage as well: the contents of those little bags will taste exactly the same night after night, every time they're served.

If you want to save money and eat well, buy fresh vegetables in season at bargain prices. Substitute frozen only when fresh are not available or when prices are prohibitive. Season them with imagination, to your taste. Do not buy them seasoned or sauced.

To sauce frozen vegetables: cook vegetables according to package directions (measure water and time accurately or they will be limp, lifeless things, not fit to eat), drain them and add what I call "butter plus." Just what "plus" is is up to you, but here are a few suggestions:

ASPARAGUS - To one package of cooked and drained frozen asparagus, add: one pat butter plus sprinkling of nutmeg, or one tablespoon heavy cream plus pinch of curry powder, or two tablespoons "homemade in a blender" mayonnaise.

LIMA BEANS - To one package of cooked and drained frozen lima beans, add: one pat butter plus one teaspoon prepared mustard or horseradish, or two tablespoons mayonnaise, or butter plus generous sprinkling dry bread crumbs (made from left over dry bread or rolls).

97

BROCCOLI - To one package of cooked and drained frozen broccoli, add: mayonnaise as above or butter plus fresh lemon juice, or grated Swiss or parmesan cheese, or crumbled sharp cheddar or blue cheese tossed with broccoli ½ minute before taking from stove.

BRUSSEL SPROUTS - To one package of cooked and drained frozen brussel sprouts, add: heavy cream plus chopped pecans, butter plus lemon juice, or grated cheese of any kind.

CAULIFLOWER - To one package of cooked and drained frozen cauliflower, add: butter plus paprika and freshly ground black pepper, or heavy cream plus grated cheese.

GREEN PEAS - To one package of cooked and drained frozen green peas, add: butter plus chopped fresh mint or chopped chives.

GREEN BEANS - To one package of cooked and drained frozen green beans, add: crumbled, cooked bacon and paper thin slices of purple onion, or butter, lemon juice and chopped chives.

SPINACH - To one package of cooked and drained frozen spinach, add: heavy cream plus grated cheese, or chopped egg yolks, chopped chives, or for a surprise contrast in texture, chopped almonds or Brazil nuts.

BEANS, PASTA, RICE
AND
SUCH

BEANS, PASTA, RICE AND SUCH

Take two cans of Mother's home-style baked beans, wrap them neatly in brown paper, tie them with sturdy white string and send them post-haste to Andy Warhol.

Now, take one pound small pea beans, put them in a bowl and cover with cold water. Let soak overnight. Place a piece of scored* salt pork (about ⅛ lb.) in the bottom of an earthenware bean pot (or any non-metal, oven-proof casserole or pot). Add beans and any water not absorbed by soaking. Pour over them ½ cup molasses, and enough water to cover. Add one chopped onion, one teaspoon dry mustard, and ¼ teaspoon paprika. Mix gently but thoroughly.** Bury a second piece of scored salt pork (same size as the first) in the center. Cover pot and bake at 300°F. for about six hours. Every now and again,*** give a look and add additional water as needed. Last hour remove lid of bean pot so surface of beans may become crisp and brown.

Cost: approximately 40 cents, yield about five cups beans, eight to ten servings. I do love that word "yield." Home economists who work for large food companies love it too. It sounds so efficient.

Cost of glass jar of baked pea beans: about 30 cents, yield per jar, 1¾ cups. (There are cheaper canned beans but how low, I mean, can you get?)

If you don't want to serve five cups beans at one time, what you don't serve can be frozen, and they will actually be better for a stay in the cold. You will want beans some time again, won't you?

P.S. To reheat baked beans takes about the same time and effort as opening and heating canned beans.

P.S. again: I'm not saying a word about the difference in flavor between home-cooked and canned beans. You be the judge. After all, some people don't have to worry about a food budget, and some people prefer the taste of perservatives in their food. There's no accounting for taste.

---

* Scored means to cut the surface with a knife. The purpose here is too keep the salt pork from curling.

** Mix gently, but thoroughly, simply means to lift the beans carefully with a spoon so the liquid and seasoning are distributed evenly among the beans and penetrate to the bottom.

*** Now and again means about every two hours. If you want to go out for three or four hours, just add a little more water than needed.

Ideally, surface of liquid in pot should remain even with beans.

While you're at it, why not also send Mr. Warhol a pre-packaged package of Italian noodles Romano? He will undoubtedly write and thank you for this superb inspiration. Just think what he can do with that small inner package of sauce mix, and how pleased you will be to receive his letter! Why, his signature alone is worth your trouble and money, which it certainly would not have been if you had prepared and eaten the stuff.

A six-ounce package of this misnamed insult to Italian cuisine costs about 49 cents. Besides noodles, it contains that small envelope of sauce mix. You add butter (one tablespoon) and milk (one cup) bringing the total cost to about 60 cents.

For about 22 cents you can buy an eight ounce package of the best domestic brand egg noodles or, at an Italian grocer, 30 to 32 cents will get you the same amount of the finest, imported from Italy fettuccini. For about 25 cents more, you can make fettuccini alla Romana, for real. It takes less money, less time and less work. It would be an understatement to say it tastes twice as good.

So, cook your fettuccini according to package directions. For really al dente, just barely tender, while it's cooking, cream together two tablespoons room temperature butter with one tablespoon anchovy paste. Mix into hot drained fettuccini. With kitchen shears, snip in four or five sprigs (well washed and well drained) parsley. Toss lightly and serve at once with lots of freshly grated Romano cheese to pass at the table. This amount will serve two hungry people as a main course, or four as a first course to be followed by fish, chicken or meat.

The mix package states its six ounces will serve four. But how parsimonious can you get?

For that matter, why not send Mr. Warhol the entire line of these pastas? This company makes, besides the noodles Romano: "Spaghetti Italy," spaghetti with tomato sauce mix, "Noodles Almondine," cream, sauce mix, and real slivered almonds (at least three whole almonds in each box), and something called "Noodle Doodle," we think, though what's in this last we really don't know. Being so thrown by the name, we were unable to pick up the package. Besides, we would have been ashamed to take it past the girl at the check out counter. Even at supermarkets, we do have our pride.

These packages are all the same price, Lordy me, about 59 cents.

Spaghetti plain, eight ounces of the best, costs less than 23 cents.

The best tomato sauce we ever had in Italy, made at home with fresh tomatoes, need not cost over 35 cents for two to four servings. That is, unless you make it when tomatoes are priced sky high. Then we suggest you make instead, some other sauce.

(You do know, we really hope you do, that fresh tomatoes contain lots of vitamin C and other things much better for you than dehydrated tomato sauce.)

For tomato sauce pure Italian style: take two or three large chopped tomatoes, put them in a saucepan, and cook over low heat until they are reduced to a pulp. Stir often. Takes about 30 minutes. No, no, do not add water, oil, butter or anything else. Now, take the pan off the heat and stir in one or two tablespoons butter and one or two tablespoons best quality olive oil. Stir until smooth, add salt, coarse ground black pepper, a dash of hot sauce and there you are, Sauce Italian Supreme. Spoon it over warm soup bowls of just-cooked hot spaghetti, rush it to the table and let each happy recipient help himself to freshly grated parmesan cheese.

Pick up a package of instant rice; instantly put it back on your grocer's shelf. It deserves even less attention, but just for the record, fast readers, give a quick look as to price and net content. Compare (in price and net content) with regular white rice, converted long grain rice, brown rice, and such "added to" and "seasoned" rices as Spanish rice, herb rice, rice and vermicelli, etc. Now, turn around and walk out of that supermarket empty handed. Go to the nearest Italian grocery store, gourmet food shop, or health food store where you will find, and buy, a package of imported Italian rice. You will then have the finest rice you can cook. It will not stick or become gummy, ever. It will taste divine; what's more, it will cost less per serving and take absolutely no more effort to prepare than that instant "hoax in a box."

Want proof? Though certainly the flavor can only be substantiated by buying, cooking and trying, the arithmetic is crystal clear and as simple as this: Precooked (so called instant) rice costs 29 cents per seven ounce package; yield per package, three cups cooked rice: cost per cup cooked rice, more than nine cents. Imported Italian rice costs 45 to 49 cents per one pound package: yield per package, eight cups cooked rice, cost per cup, five to six cents per cup.

As to effort and time:

To cook imported Italian rice bring four cups water to full boil, slowly pour in one cup rice, stir once. Add about ⅓ teaspoon salt and ½ teaspoon butter or oil. Turn heat low and allow rice to simmer gently until all but the last bit of water has evaporated from the bottom of the pan.* Turn off heat and cover pan. In about a minute or less, each grain will be separated, dry, fluffy, delicious and ready to serve.

While on the subject of rice, perhaps it's a good time to take a quick run down as to price, nutritional value and ease in cooking of the various type rices you will find on your grocer's shelf. However, before we begin, let me stress these points: No rice is difficult to cook, none take very long to prepare and all are new-wife-proof and fool-proof as well, if you will follow the very simple package directions.

White Rice: price depends on brand and quality; can be anywhere from 19 to 25 cents per one pound package. However, the less expensive brands may prove to be gummy and sticky and can also be somewhat flat in flavor. In addition they are a poor buy in nutritional value; rice is devitalized when minerals and vitamins are removed by refining and are not replaced.

"Converted" or "enriched" long grain rice: price per one pound package: 27 to 29 cents. Next to Italian rice, your best buy in price, nutritional value, flavor and texture.

Brown Rice: price per pound: 25 to 27 cents. Excellent flavor and nutritional value. It tends, however, to be gummy and sticky and takes much longer to cook than white rice. But we hasten to add again, no more actual work is involved.

---

* This takes about twenty minutes. You can use the time to watch TV, have a cocktail, powder your nose, or you can set your table and complete preparation on the balance of your meal, which of course you will have to do anyway, no matter what type of rice you cook.

Seasoned and "added to" rices such as herb rice, Spanish rice, curried rice, etc: 39 to 44 cents per six ounce package! Ridiculous to even contemplate. You can make your own seasoned rices with very little effort and only a few pennies additional cost over plain white rice.

HERB RICE

(4 to 6 servings)

3 tablespoons butter
2 tablespoons finely chopped onion
1 cup Italian or long grain converted or enriched rice
¼ teaspoon dried thyme
1 bay leaf
2 sprigs parsley
2 drops Tabasco sauce
1½ cups rich chicken stock (see recipe for stock page 48)
2½ cups water

Melt butter in a deep heavy sauce pan, add onions, cook, stirring until transparent. Add rice and stir two minutes longer. Add thyme, bay leaf, parsley, Tabasco, stock and water. Bring to boil over high heat, stir once. Reduce heat to very low, let rice simmer very gently, uncovered, until all but the last bit of water has evaporated. Remove from heat, cover pan, let stand one to two minutes covered. Remove parsley and serve.

Cost: about 23 cents (with regular rice). Cost: 35 cents (with Italian rice).

PILAU

---

3 tablespoons butter
1 small chopped onion
1 small clove garlic, finely chopped (optional)
1 cup Italian imported or converted long grain white rice
Salt to taste - ½ to 1 teaspoon
5 cups boiling chicken or beef stock or water
¼ cup sultana raisins (optional)
¼ cup chopped almonds (optional)

Melt butter in a heavy sauce pan, add onion and garlic. Cook over low heat until soft. Add rice. Continue stirring until golden, add salt to taste. Stir to blend. Pour on boiling water, cover pan partially with lid, let simmer over very low heat until all liquid is absorbed and rice is tender. Stir in raisins and almonds, if desired.

Cost: 45 cents (with regular rice). Cost: 55 cents (with Italian rice). (Almonds and raisins are not in packaged, already seasoned rice.)

CURRIED RICE

(Serves 4 to 6)

2 tablespoons butter
1 tablespoon finely chopped shallots or scallions
1 to 2 teaspoons curry powder
1½ cups long grain imported Italian or converted white rice*
½ teaspoon salt
¼ cup dry white wine
4 cups water, or chicken or beef stock

Melt butter in a heavy sauce pan, add shallots or scallions. Cook over low heat until soft. Blend in curry powder, add rice, stir until golden. Add wine and salt, cook until absorbed. Add water or stock. Cook over low heat until this liquid is also absorbed (about 20 minutes).

Cost: about 35 cents (with regular rice). Cost: about 45 cents (with Italian rice).

* If using domestic rice, rinse before cooking in several changes of cold water, then soak for one hour in cold water and drain thoroughly.

FRIED RICE

(Serves 4 to 6)

⅓ cup oil
3 cups cooked Italian or long grain white rice
2 eggs (slightly beaten)
1 scallion (finely chopped)
¼ cup finely minced or chopped cooked ham, chicken, beef, crabmeat, lobster or crumbled bacon (whatever's on hand).
¼ cup thinly sliced water chestnuts or almonds (optional)
1 to 2 tablespoons soy sauce

Heat oil in large heavy skillet, add rice, stir with fork or spatula (about three minutes) until golden. Push rice away from center of pan to form a hollow, pour in eggs, stir into rice. Continue "frying" over low heat, stirring often, until rice separates again and is completely dry. Use spatula to keep "scraping up" dry eggs from bottom of pan. Stir in remaining ingredients. Cook, stirring two minutes longer.

Cost: 52 cents (about ¼ the price of frozen fried rice-49 cents for two servings!).

MIXES
NOT FOR MAKING

MIXES NOT FOR MAKING

Buy two packages of biscuit mix and two packages of pie crust mix from your grocer this very week. Use them, but really, use them up somehow. Make pies, fried turnovers, pancakes, dumplings, coffee cake and any other concoction suggested on the package labels. (If you run out of recipes, turn to your ladies', so-called home service magazine where you're sure to find more, like maybe meat roley poleys, and frankfurter doughnuts). Repeat your purchases and "cooking" each week. Serve something made with them at every meal. This will enable you to cut down on portions of meat, fresh vegetables and fruit.

We call this murder by the packaged mix method, or the perfect crime. It may take time, but it's sure. In fact, this is for you if you want to do away with the old (husband, that is), collect the insurance, and marry the new husband without being suspected, investigated by the police, or politely shown to a neat little room at the county jail.

After all, who could suspect thrifty good cookin' you, all the time baking and frying up special goodies just for your husband's pleasure and not caring one little bit if he lost his waistline and slept off a too heavy meal every night instead of taking you to Michael Caine movies.

Certainly you won't tell anyone after, or for that matter, before the sad event, that you knew all the time about the damage caused to the health of any man forced (unwittingly or otherwise) to eat large quantities of hydrogenated shortening at every meal, abundant in both these mixes. Or how you were aware that these products were made from little more than refined white flour, chemical fresheners and preservatives which would add to unhealthy overweight, but would supply very little, if any, nutrition. Most certainly, you will not brag about how you shopped around town looking for torn and worn packages of the stuff knowing that it left too long on a grocer's shelf, it could and did become rancid, and that the rancid shortening would cause your husband severe vitamin deficiencies which, in turn, would make him susceptible to any disease, with a constitution too weak to resist or throw off infection.

Certainly not, no indeedy deed, not "now insurance rich" and happy little you. You were smart enough to have eaten very little of what you cooked. You can throw away any leftover evidence and concentrate instead on keeping healthy by making only such breads and biscuits that are good for you.

Only incidentally, it can't make much difference now that those insurance checks keep rolling in, but "good for you" baked and even fried foods need cost very little more to make than those made from a mix. Though they do indeed sometimes take as much as five minutes more to prepare, they taste like what they are, homemade.

BISCUITS

1   cup all purpose flour
1½   cups whole wheat flour (stone ground)
1   teaspoon salt
3   teaspoons baking powder
      pinch of soda
3   tablespoon lard, chilled
2½   tablespoons butter, chilled
¾   cup cold milk

Preheat oven to 450° F.

Combine flours, salt, baking powder and soda. Cut in lard and butter with a pastry cutter until mixture resembles coarse ground cornmeal. Add milk all at once to dry ingredients, and with floured hands quickly form mixture into a soft dough. Turn out onto a lightly floured board and roll out to ½" thickness. Cut with floured biscuit cutter.

Place on ungreased baking sheet and bake (in preheated 450°F. oven) until lightly browned, 10 to 12 minutes.

Reread the first two sentences. This is the extra work needed to make homemade, instead of made from a mix, biscuits.

The difference in flavor and nutrition resulting from the use of whole wheat flour is something else again. Rather like the difference between last night's reheated pork chops and today's just-from-the-pan bacon. Only more so.

PANCAKES

(about 18 medium size cakes)

Made from a mix, you add one egg to two cups of mix. Result: heavy and fattening. Homemade, you add three eggs to 1 (one) cup flour. Result: light, less fattening, delicious, and much better for your health.

Difficult? What's difficult about it?

GOURMET PANCAKES
(Breakfast Crepes)

1½	cups milk
3	eggs
2	tablespoons soft butter (room temperature)
¾	cup flour
1	teaspoon baking powder
½	teaspoon salt
½	teaspoon sugar

Dump all ingredients in order listed, into electric blender. Blend at high speed until smooth, or put ingredients in mixing bowl and beat with wire whisk until smooth. Let stand about 15 minutes. Pour from mixer container, or spoon from bowl, about two tablespoons batter into lightly greased small crepe pan. Cook until bubbly on top, turn and brown underside. Makes 18 to 20 medium size crepes.

SAVE YOUR HUSBAND
MUFFINS

¾   cup stoneground whole wheat flour
⅓   cup all purpose white flour
¼   teaspoon salt
1   tablespoon sugar
2   teaspoons baking powder
    pinch of soda
¾   cup milk
3   large eggs, lightly beaten
2   tablespoons melted butter

Preheat oven to 375°F.

Mix together dry ingredients. Stir in remaining ingredients. Pour into lightly greased muffin tins. Bake in preheated 375°F. oven until firm, 12 to 15 minutes. Makes about one dozen muffins.

NON-LETHAL APPLE "PIE"
(Really Apple Betty)

This tastes just as good (in fact far better) as sure 'nuff apple pie, but the difference is that each delicious mouthful adds to, not subtracts from, your health. But forget about the health aspect; it's heavenly to taste and almost as easy as heating a frozen pie, to say nothing of costing far less.

6   medium size tart apples
1   cup brown sugar
1½   cups wheat germ
     grated rind of ½ lemon
3   tablespoons butter

Peel and core apples. Mix sugar, wheat germ and lemon rind together. Now, slice apples and place a layer in an oven proof casserole, cover with wheat germ-sugar mixture. Repeat with another layer of apples until all ingredients are used, topping with a layer of wheat germ-sugar. Dot with butter and bake in a 350° F. oven, 30 to 45 minutes, until apples are tender and "crust" is nicely browned. Serve with heavy cream.

CORNBREAD NOT TO DIE FOR

Real honest-go-goodness natural cornmeal can be found in health food stores and it's well worth looking for. Not only does the cornbread taste infinitely better, but it's far, far better for you. Commercial cornmeal is something else again, something to forget about (like corn bread mixes), unless you really do have mayhem on your mind.

1½   cups natural yellow cornmeal
½   cup flour
1   teaspoon baking powder
1   teaspoon salt
1   teaspoon sugar (optional)
3   eggs
1   cup milk
¼   cup melted butter

Preheat oven to 400° F. Grease a shallow baking pan and place in oven to heat. Combine cornmeal, flour, baking powder and salt in a mixing bowl. Add eggs, milk and cooled melted butter. Beat well to blend. Pour in preheated pan and bake 20 to 25 minutes until lightly browned.

PIE CRUST

Made from a mix - mix the mix with water, roll out on floured board, fit into pie tin, fill, bake. Eating is optional.

PIE CRUST HOMEMADE

Don't! It's fattening and it's bad for your health. Better desserts, and better for you, may be made for less money and in less time.

JUST COOKIES

JUST COOKIES

Bring home a package of cookies, the deluxe, "all buttery" old fashioned, grandmotherly kind that comes so charmingly packaged twelve to the bag. They will have cost you about half a dollar, give or take a penny or two, but no matter; the outer wrapping alone is worth your outlay of cash. Framed and hung in your kitchen, it will make a gay little print. As to the contents, well, no price is too high when it comes to giving your children the best - education - and these little rounds of mostly flour and sugar* really can be of great help.

Unwrap the package and place the cookies on a low table. Call the little ones and tell them to bring their little slates. Seat them round about and, making of the entire proceedings a gay little game**, bid them ascertain the answer

---

* All butter cookies are not as the name seems to imply, "all butter." They are still, as other commercial cookies, mostly all flour, sugar, artificial flavor and preservatives. True, no other shortening is used, but the ratio of butter to cookies is anyone's guesss.

** The packaged cookies will be uneatable after handling, but no matter, they were more than likely uneatable to begin with.

to this simple sum. If one dozen cookies cost 48 cents, how much will it cost to buy a dozen cookies each week for a full year? Give the first child to answer correctly a motherly kiss (isn't this all rather nauseating, though?), one or two homemade cookies * and a small mug of milk.

If they are particularly bright little things, you might proceed with a puzzle like this: if eight dozen cookies take only about one hour to make and cost as little as five or ten cents a dozen, why the hell would anyone be so foolish as to buy eight dozen cookies at a cost of $3.04?

Obviously, with this type of loaded question, one must be prepared for the precocious child's answer which might precociously be to the effect that Mother, having read "Feminine Mystique," is not really the cookie making type, and anyway, just doesn't have time, what with the P.T.A., her bridge club and being hung over both Saturday and Sunday mornings.

But this is not of course correct, heaven forbid, and the little thing should be rebuked and set right.

Cookie buyers are simply people who read, but do not think. Even a mama mini-bopper will change her style (for the time it takes to "make," not buy) if the arithmetic is made clear.

---

* If you build up your story, you'll have the kids so carried away by the idea that they will be wild to make cookies. So why not? There are more ways than one to skin a budget. Besides, they really will have fun and even little old "Mystique" you might want to join in.

    If you buy one box of one dozen cookies at 48 cents each week for a year, you will have spent $24.96. If you make them at home at ten cents a dozen (and this is easily done), the cost will drop (for 52 dozen cookies) to $5.20. The savings thus effected will be $19.76 or ample cash to buy a new mini skirt, a pair of tall, shiny, plastic rain boots, a night on the town or, to be just a bit more plebian, a new toilet seat, if that's what's needed in a particular house.

    Besides, and do explain this to your little monsters (there's a reason), making cookies is child's play, and can even be pleasant and fun. We add, only as an afterthought of course, but it is important to those people whose taste buds have not been dulled by artificial flavor and preservatives, "home made" cookies taste better than "boughten" and they are also better for your health.

Did we say five to ten cents a dozen? Yes, dear girl, we did. Here are a few examples. Leaf through any good, old-fashioned cook book and you'll find half a hundred more.

LACE COOKIES

You won't find them at your supermarket

2	tablespoons butter
1½	cups sugar
3	eggs
½	teaspoon salt
1	teaspoon vanilla
3½	cups uncooked oatmeal
4	teaspoons baking powder

Preheat oven to 300°F.

Butter baking sheet generously.

Place butter in a large sauce pan over low heat until melted. Remove from heat and stir in sugar. Add eggs and beat a full minute. Add remaining ingredients in order listed. Drop by the spoonful onto prepared baking sheet. Bake (in preheated 300°F. oven) for eight to ten minutes or until lightly browned. Remove from pan at once.

125

Makes about five dozen cookies. Cost: about 50 cents.

BROWNIES
(For Real)

---

4   tablespoons butter
2   squares (2 ounces) unsweetened chocolate
1   tablespoon strong coffee (save it from breakfast)
1   cup sugar
2   large eggs
1   cup flour
⅛   teaspoon salt
½   teaspoon baking powder
¾   cup finely chopped walnuts
1   teaspoon vanilla
    confectioners' sugar

Preheat oven to 325°F.

Butter a 9″ cake pan. Place butter and chocolate in a large sauce pan or metal mixing bowl over very low heat until melted. Remove from heat, stir in coffee, then sugar, and beat a half-minute. Add eggs and beat a final half-minute.

Sift flour, salt and baking powder onto waxed paper.

Add to above ingredients in mixing bowl. Mix in nuts. Stir until blended. Stir in vanilla.

Pour into prepared pan and bake 30 to 35 minutes. Let cool in pan, then cut into strips. Roll strips in confectioners' sugar.

Makes about three dozen. Cost: about 75 cents.

Cost of brownie mix: about 39 cents, but then you have to add the nuts, and the result of your efforts will be about one dozen brownie squares, small ones.

CREOLE MACAROONS

2   cups light brown sugar
2   cups pecans, finely ground
2   egg whites
¾   cup confectioners' sugar

Thoroughly mix all ingredients except confectioners' sugar. Divide and roll into small balls. Bake 2″ apart on ungreased baking sheet at 350° F. for 10 to 15 minutes. Roll in confectioners' sugar while still warm. Makes about eight dozen cookies.

Cost: about 80 cents.

BUTTER COOKIES

½   pound butter (room temperature)
1   cup white sugar (or ½ cup white sugar and ½ cup brown sugar)
1   large egg
1   teaspoon almond extract
2¼   cups flour
1   teaspoon double-acting baking powder
⅛   teaspoon salt
    additional flour as needed

Cream butter with sugar. Beat in egg and almond extract. Add flour, baking powder and salt, and stir to a stiff dough.

Transfer dough to a well-floured double-thick piece of wax paper (do not wrap paper around dough). Place in freezing compartment of refrigerator for about 30 minutes or until well chilled and firm.

With lightly floured hands, form dough (still on waxed paper) into a long log, about 2″ in diameter. Divide roll in half and wrap each half in lightly floured waxed paper. Refrigerate or freeze until ready to bake.

Preheat oven to 350°F.

With a sharp knife cut roll into thin rounds. Place on ungreased cookie sheet and bake eight to ten minutes or until edges are lightly browned.

Makes about seven dozen cookies. Cost: about 65 cents.

The price of Butter Cookies at my local bakery is $2.10 per pound. Yes, it is a great bakery but their products are still not up to those of my own kitchen, and you know how many cookies it takes to make one pound? About four dozen, that's how many, at a cost of more than 52 cents per dozen.

Note: unused dough may be stored in your freezer or freezing compartment of your refrigerator up to one month.

Baked cookies may be stored in an air tight container up to one week.

BUTTER NUT COOKIES

Add ½ to one cup chopped walnuts, pecans or peanuts (unsalted, natch) to basic butter cookie batter before chilling.

CHOCOLATE COOKIES

Stir in two squares (two ounces) melted and cooled unsweetened chocolate to butter cookie batter before adding flour, baking powder and salt.

LEMON COOKIES

Substitute one tablespoon lemon juice for almond extract in basic butter cookie recipe. Stir in one tablespoon grated lemon rind before chilling dough.

SPICE COOKIES

Eliminate almond extract, add one teaspoon instant coffee, ½ teaspoon cinnamon and ¼ teaspoon nutmeg to batter and blend well before adding flour, baking powder and salt.

ANISE-SEED COOKIES

Substitute vanilla for almond extract and add one teaspoon pulverized anise seeds to basic butter cookie batter.

CINNAMON SUGAR COOKIES

Sprinkle cut cookies before baking with sugar and cinnamon.

BUTTER RUM COOKIES

Substitute one tablespoon dark rum for almond extract in basic butter cookie recipe.

GINGERSNAPS

Unlike mother used to buy

¼   pound butter, cut into cubes
½   cup molasses
⅓   cup brown sugar, packed down
1   teaspoon powdered ginger
1   teaspoon powdered cinnamon
2   tablespoons dark rum
1   teaspoon baking soda
2½   cups all-purpose flour

In a large (but *large*, you're going to make the dough in this pan) saucepan, put butter, molasses and sugar. Place over low heat until butter and sugar have melted. (Stir now and again.) Add ginger, cinnamon, rum and baking soda, and blend. Remove from heat and let cool to lukewarm. Then stir in flour.

Transfer dough to a well floured double-thick sheet of waxed paper and place in freezing compartment of refrigerator until chilled and firm.

Preheat oven to 350°F.

Grease baking sheet.

Roll out about 1/5 dough very thin on a lightly floured board. Cut with 2″ to 2½″ cookie cutter. Place on greased baking sheet and bake eight to ten minutes or until firm.

Repeat until all dough has been used.

Makes about nine dozen small cookies. Cost: about 70 cents.

Note: Homemade gingersnaps will keep fresh and crisp (in an air tight container) two to three weeks, about twice as long as boxed gingersnaps.

JUST DESSERTS

JUST DESSERTS

Buy that package of new new new real egg custard mix. The company that just brought it out has such high hopes for its success. Why, even the package has the color of real egg. It costs only about 33 cents and it's soooo easy and quick; just add milk (3 cups) and one fresh egg yolk, mix, heat, stir to boiling, pour into serving dishes and chill, but thoroughly. This last is important, however, because if it is not really cold, you are apt to taste the trisodium citrate, calcium carrageenan, or the sodium silico aluminate as well as the non fat dry skim milk, sugar, and egg yolk solids. Not particularly pleasant things these, no indeed.

It would be better, perhaps, if dessert must be ready in less time, to simply make Spanish flan which is not new (Spanish housewives have been preparing it for years), but can be served warm if necessary, and it does cost just a little bit less.

The total cost of preparing egg custard mix custard: 54 cents. Cost of homemade flan: 39 cents.

(Based on milk at 28 cents a quart, eggs at 60 cents per dozen, sugar at 50 cents per five-pound bag, vanilla at 21 cents per bottle.)

You can also, it says so right on the box, make a similar (looking) dessert to flan with this mix, but it's more work than "homemade," and besides it will cost, based on the above figures, 61 cents.

FLAN

---

4   tablespoons sugar plus ⅓ cup sugar
4   eggs
1   teaspoon vanilla
2   cups milk

Place four tablespoons sugar in an oven proof casserole, one that may also be used over direct heat. Cook over very low flame until sugar has turned to a light golden syrup. Remove from fire, tilt pan to coat sides with syrup, set aside to cool. Combine eggs, milk, ⅓ cup sugar and vanilla. Blend with wire whisk or fork and pour into cooled casserole. Set casserole in a slightly larger pan containing water to within one inch of custard. Bake at 325°F. for thirty minutes or until custard has set. Chilled, it's lovely, but it's just as good warm.

P.S. You can make the sugar syrup in a saucepan, then pour it into a ring mold or custard cup and proceed as above.

The French also serve an egg custard with caramelized sauce not from a mix. However, they put the sugar on top instead of on the bottom, and more than likely it's light brown. It's called creme brulé, and at most elegant French restaurants it's priced at about a dollar a serving. You can make it at home for less than the price of real egg custard.

CREME BRULÉ

4	eggs
⅓	cup white sugar
1	teaspoon vanilla
2	cups warm (scalded) milk
½	cup light brown sugar

Beat egg with fork or wire whisk until frothy. Beat in white sugar, then slowly add milk and vanilla beating constantly. Continue beating until smooth. Pour into lightly buttered mold or individual custard cups. Place in baking pan containing water to within one inch of custard cups. Bake at 325°F. until set. Chill thoroughly. When ready to serve, sprinkle surface with the brown sugar making sure none of the custard shows through. Set in a pan of ice water to within one inch of custard cups and place directly under high broiler flame until sugar caramelizes. It takes less than a minute so watch carefully or the sugar will burn. Serve at once while the "sauce" is bubbly hot, and the custard still icy cold.

P.S. For simple egg custard use the above recipe increasing

white sugar to ½ cup and omitting brown sugar topping. Just sprinkle lightly with nutmeg and bake, then serve warm, at room temperature or well chilled. It will cost you all of 45 cents, again less than "made from a mix" egg custard, and it's actually less trouble to make. P.S. again: It contains less sugar, more eggs, and no preservatives. We leave you the task of figuring out the nutritional advantage all by yourself.

The cooks of southern Louisiana again use these same ingredients for a custard, but come up with something else entirely. They call it creme caramel. Its poor relation can be made with caramel custard mix, but it bears very little family resemblance and, honestly, why should you when the real thing costs only about ten cents additional and five minutes more to home bake. Besides, it tastes like a light hearted dream, not starch, sugar and artificial flavoring.

LOUISIANA CREME CARAMEL

1½ cups sugar
4   tablespoons water
⅛   teaspoon cream of tartar
4   eggs
1   teaspoon vanilla
2   cups warm (scalded) milk

Combine sugar, water, and cream of tartar in saucepan. Cook over low heat until it turns to a light golden syrup. Set aside to cool slightly while you beat the eggs until frothy. Then slowly pour in syrup, beating constantly. Add vanilla and milk and continue beating until smooth (sounds like a lot of beating but it takes only a minute or less). Pour into lightly buttered and sugared custard mold or cups. Place in a pan containing water to within one inch of custard cups. Bake at 325°F. until firm, about 30 minutes. Chill and serve. If you must be super elegant, top with whipped cream studded with toasted almonds.

RECIPES TO EAT OUT BY

Phony Spumoni

(From a recent issue of a nationally distributed magazine dedicated to better families and homes.)

You will need: sugar, hydrogenated vegetable oils with BHA, propylene glycol, monestearate, lactos, sodium casanate, whey solids, hydrolysated lecithin, sodium silico aluminate, artificial flavor and color (or one package of dessert topping mix), one tablespoon chopped candied orange peel, one tablespoon chopped almonds (toasted) ⅓ cup red and green maraschino cherries, one quart vanilla ice cream, ½ cup whipping cream and four to six large gum drops, a mixing bowl, a measuring cup, a rotary beater, a large wooden spoon, a six-cup mold, but only ten minutes, or so says the originator of this recipe. If you discount the time spent waiting for the ice cream to soften to spreading consistency, whipping the cream, cutting the gum drops into flower shapes, and decorating your finished "phony" plus washing up, she's right, dead right. However, time saved is not always money earned or so they say (though not so much anymore), and this lovely concoction will cost you about one dollar and seventy five cents. In addition, if you are having Italian guests for dinner, you might just be embarrassed.

Better to take them out for the meal, or serve a real Italian dessert, which phony spumoni is not. Indeed, the food editor who dreamed up this dish has made a lamentable

mistake, understandable when one is unfamiliar with the cuisine of a country (on my first trip to Paris, I asked for, even insisted on, a very good, very dry Sauterne*), but unfortunate in a magazine of national distribution. It does seem this girl should have "boned up" or found out before going to press. The spumoni she copied, made up and photographed in color is not spumoni as served in Italy (except perhaps for a few restaurants catering to tourists), but spumoni ice cream as made commercially here in the states.

*In France, sauterne is a sweet wine; in the U.S. it is a dry wine.

SPUMONI REAL

If you serve spumoni real, you will need:

1   cup cream
1   cup sugar
1   cup water
1   1½″ piece of vanilla bean
4   egg yolks
2   egg whites
¼   teaspoon salt
⅓   cup mixed chopped candied fruit
2   tablespoons chopped blanched almonds

Whip cream until stiff, beat in half the sugar, refrigerate. Boil water with remaining sugar and vanilla bean for three minutes. Remove vanilla bean. Beat yolks until light and "lemony." Slowly add sugar-water syrup, beating constantly. In a separate bowl, beat egg whites with salt until they stand in stiff peaks, fold in beaten cream and egg yolk mixture. Add chopped fruit and almonds, blend until smooth and pour into lightly oiled spumoni (or any one-quart) mold. Freeze 12 hours or longer.

To serve: Holding by rim, dip mold in pan of hot water 30 seconds. Turn out onto serving plate. No decoration needed, honest! If you would serve it Italian.

Oh yes, it will cost you about $1.05. Each recipe serves six to eight.

CAKE MIXES
AND
MIXING CAKES

CAKE MIXES AND MIXING CAKES

Consider the case for packaged cake mixes. Seriously, of course. Each maker of this product most certainly does, as does the advertising agency who handles his account, the public relations firm who "projects" his product's image, the artists (plural, there are dozens of them) who "create" his packaging, the chemists who perfect his formula, and the home economist who must use it each month in xxx number of recipes to be sent broadside to magazine and newspaper food editors throughout these United States and (usually) Canada as well.

Consider then!!!! How could we not?!!

Their virtues are sung on radio and demonstrated on TV each day, day in and day out, from the first morning news to the late show's last bitter end. Their recipes are on the food pages of every newspaper, and their glowing ads tempt (or attempt to tempt) us from the pages of every magazine we pick up.

They are convenient, convenient, convenient, we are told: "quick mixing" and easy. They are less expensive, and their "buttery," "eggy," or "chocolatey" flavor is just like back home. What's more, and here's the real "clincher," the punch line so to speak, they are just like Mother, or was it Grandmother?, used to take hours to bake!

Well! You know what, pardon our doubting nature but, like Shakespeare said, or was it Mary Margaret McBride, we do think that they protest just a bit too much.

Because why? Why, because no matter how you slice it, ice it, "add to" or cover it with jet spray cream topping, a cake made from a mix bears only slight resemblance in flavor and texture to a cake made "for real" from fresh eggs and butter, whole milk or cream, and what's more, the longer you keep it the less it will. Cake mix cakes taste stale if kept for more than one day. In addition, and it's a down right sad thing that this simple truth has been almost buried and lost under an avalanche of cake mix maker claims, a home "made from scratch" cake need be no more difficult or time consuming to make. The cost can be approximately the same, unless you prefer that it be less, and if desired it can be made to add to, not subtract from, your health.

Now what more could you ask? The "how to," that's all, and no postage or box top needed. Here is just that, not a new, exciting, completely original recipe, only a very old one slightly revised, that will make a truly satisfying, good, rich, smooth textured, basic cake. It may be added to or changed just a bit: made into muffins, loaf cake or layers, filled any number of ways, iced, served sugar dusted or plain. It will "keep" if wrapped properly for any number of days, and it tastes like a cake, an honest to goodness real cake.

145

SPICE CAKE

(In one bowl just like a mix)

½   pound (1 cup) butter (room temperature)
2   cups brown sugar, packed down
6   eggs
1   teaspoon powdered cinnamon
1   teaspoon powdered nutmeg
1   teaspoon grated lemon rind
3½   cups cake flour
1   cup milk
½   cup Sauterne (sweet)
1   tablespoon baking powder
      confectioners' sugar

Preheat oven to 350°F.

Lightly grease a 9″ angel food tube pan.

In large mixing bowl, cream butter with sugar. Add eggs and beat (with wire whisk) until mixture is light and fluffy. Beat in cinnamon, nutmeg and lemon rind. Add flour alternately with milk, beating well after each addition. Add Sauterne. Then, lastly add baking powder and beat thirty seconds.

Pour into prepared pan and bake (in 350°F. oven) one hour or until cake tester inserted in center comes out clean.

Remove from oven and let stand ten minutes. Remove from pan onto cake rack and let cool.

Wrap in foil and store in refrigerator until ready to serve.

Dust with confectioners' sugar just before serving.

Makes, but what else, one 9″ high, lovely spice cake.

Cost: about $1.50.

Cost of spice cake mix: about 39 cents, plus needed extra ingredients, about 10 cents, plus very needed icing, about 25 cents. Total about 74 cents. Oh dear, for once you'll spend more money, but there's this compensation. You save all that work of making an icing. Our cake doesn't need one and, besides, it's just a bit more interesting in taste, and it's so much richer it will serve twice as many.

EASIER THAN A MIX LAYER CAKE

2	cups flour
1	tablespoon baking powder
¼	teaspoon salt
¼	pound (½ cup) butter (room temperature and very soft)
1	cup sugar
2	large eggs
½	cup milk
2	tablespoons cognac or other good dry brandy

Preheat oven to 375°F.

Grease two 8″ layer pans. Dust lightly with flour, then shake out excess flour.

Sift flour, baking powder and salt into mixing bowl. Add remaining ingredients and beat like crazy (in other words, until light and smooth).

Pour into prepared pans and bake in 375° F. oven for about 20 minutes or until firm and edges are lightly browned.

Makes, obviously, two layers, which you can put together with whatever your little heart (and appetite) desires.

Use crushed and sweetened berries, instead of icing, bananas or pineapple for filling, and top with sweetened whipped cream or soft ice cream. Easier and better, don't you agree?

Note: If you are all out of cognac or brandy, substitute Bourbon whiskey, or if you must, one tablespoon milk and one tablespoon any flavoring like almond extract or vanilla.

Cost: about 45 cents. Cost of layer cake mix: about 39 cents, plus cost of extra ingredients needed, about 15 cents, total: 54 cents.

CHOCOLATE LOAF CAKE

Just like a mix, only one pan to wash, but surprise! Unlike a mix, it's so rich and moist it doesn't need icing and it keeps for days or, if frozen, for weeks (if it's not eaten, that is).

¼ pound (1 stick) butter
4 squares (4 ounces) unsweetened chocolate
½ cup water
2 cups sugar
2 cups cake flour
2 tablespoons boiling water
3 eggs
2 tablespoons Bourbon whiskey
2 teaspoons baking powder
 pinch of salt

Cut butter in several pieces and combine it in a large (but large) sauce pan or in a metal mixing bowl with cholate and water. Place over very low heat until chocolate and butter have melted. Stir to blend, then remove from heat and let cool slightly. Add sugar and beat well. Then, add flour and continue to beat until batter is smooth. Cover and refrigerate six to eight hours or overnight.

Preheat oven to 350°F.

Remove batter from refrigerator. Add boiling water and beat until no longer stiff. Add eggs and beat until well-blended and smooth. Stir in Bourbon, then baking powder and salt. Pour into well greased and lightly floured loaf pan and bake (at 350°F.) for one hour or until cake shrinks from side of pan.

Let stand about five minutes. Loosen cake from sides of pan with a table knife, then turn out onto a cake rack to cool.

Cost: about 80 cents; no icing needed. Cost of cake mix chocolate cake: about 49 cents, plus extra needed ingredients, about 12 cents, plus icing mix (if it's to have any resemblance to a rich cake) 25 cents. Total 86 cents.

Note: No, you do not have to cream the butter, beat eggs separately or sift flour. Yes, you do have to beat this batter. As we said, it's just like a mix, but easier.

Note Again: This is the cake I sold in my posh little gourmet kitchen shop on the posh little East Side of posh little old New York for $5.00 per cake. The New York Times gave it rave reviews. I couldn't make enough cakes to supply the demand.

FRUIT CAKE

(Like you can't buy in a pretty tin box)

1	cup butter (room temperature)
1	cup sugar
5	egg yolks
3	cups cake flour
2	tablespoons dark rum
1½	cups raisins
¾	cup chopped walnuts
1	4-ounce jar diced preserved citron
5	egg whites
½	cup light rum

Preheat oven to 350 F.

Grease a 10″ x 5″ x 3″ loaf pan. Line bottom with waxed paper. Grease paper and dust lightly with flour.

Place butter in mixing bowl. Add sugar and blend until light and fluffy. Add egg yolks and beat well. Stir in flour then rum, raisins, walnuts and citron.

In a separate bowl, beat egg whites until stiff but not dry. Fold them into the batter. Pour batter immediately into prepared pan. Bake 1½ hours or until cake separates easily from sides of pan when pressed with fingertips.

Remove from oven and let stand ten minutes. Turn out onto cake rack to cool.

When cool enough to handle, place in a shallow pan and with a small, sharp knife make several slashes in the top of the cake. Then slowly pour ½ cup rum over the surface. Drain off any rum that is not absorbed by the cake and repeat until all rum is absorbed.

Wrap cake first in a clean linen napkin, then in foil, and store for several days before enjoying.

Cost: about $1.50. Cost of similar (?) fruit cake in a fancy "Christmasy" tin box: $2.50 to $5.00.

RECIPES TO EAT OUT BY

A Brilliant Party Dessert

(From a recently published cook book on time-and-money-saving "convenience" foods.)

You will need: two packages of frozen mixed fruit, one cake mix, two eggs, one package of unflavored geletin, ½ pint heavy cream, butter, flour and confectioners' sugar, one bowl, another bowl, a strainer, another bowl, a mixing spoon, a measuring cup, two cake pans, cake racks, sharp knife, wax paper, cake plate, another measuring cup, a double boiler, another bowl, another bowl, a wire whisk, a rotary beater, another spoon, knife again, spoon again, and approximately three hours.

It's called Butterfly Wings (serves six to eight). Cost: about $1.50.

Shall we eat out, or maybe instead, prepare Strawberries au Kirsch? This can be called a brilliant party dessert, but never Butterfly Wings.

You will need: two pints strawberries, three tablespoons sugar, three to four tablespoons Kirsch, a colander, a spoon and a serving bowl. Hull strawberries into colander, rinse under cold running water, transfer to serving bowl. Sprinkle with sugar, add Kirsch, toss gently. Let "mellow" for about one hour before serving. (Serves six to eight.)

Cost depends on price of strawberries. At 40 cents per pint: about $1.10.

Note: When this fruit goes over 59 cents per pint, we are inspired to serve something else.

AND NOW WHAT...

Mary Jane Suburb quickly slipped into her one-piece zip suit and dashed to her jet stream car. In no time at all she was hurrying through the neat aisles of her nearby super-market. "Let's see, have I forgotten anything?" she mused to herself as she swiftly glanced down the list in her hand. "Minute steak, quick, quick rice, heat and eat prebuttered butter beans, instant pop popovers, and hasty pudding. I guess that's all if I'm going to take advantage of the five item limit, quick check-out counter."

Meanwhile, back in the city, her husband John efficiently cleared his desk of the day's business (he was an efficiency expert) and being a man who never minced words said, "bye" to his secretary and quickly walked the three short blocks to the station and his 5:22 express train.

"Your timing is perfect," Mary said, exactly 49 minutes later as, with a quick smile, she helped him off with his coat. "If you hurry, you have almost seven minutes to relax and drink your ready-mix martini before dinner."

"Well," said John, 17 minutes later, "that was great, I don't think Mother ever fixed a faster meal."

"Yes," said his wife, "and I'll have the table cleared and the throw-away dishes thrown away in less than two minutes."

"Great," smiled John, pleased with his wife's efficiency. Then suddenly his face fell.

"But, what'll we do now?"

INDEX

SALAD DRESSINGS

ENTREES

VEGETABLES

BISCUITS, ETC.

DESSERTS

NORMAL SEASONAL AVAILABILITY – NATIONWIDE
FRESH FRUIT AND VEGETABLES

COMMODITY	SEASONAL AVAILABILITY	COMMODITY	SEASONAL AVAILABILITY
APPLES	year-round (mostly Oct.-March) peak: Sept.-Nov.	CARROTS	year-round
APRICOTS	April-mid Aug. peak: June-July	CAULIFLOWER	year-round peak: Oct.-Dec.
ARTICHOKES	Sept.-July peak: March-April	CELERY	year-round peak: Nov.-May
ASPARAGUS	March-June peak: April-May	CHERRIES	May-Aug. peak: June
AVOCADOS	year-round peak: July-Sept.	COLLARDS	year-round peak: Jan.-Feb.
BEANS,GREEN	year-round peak: March-Aug.	CORN,GREEN	April-Oct. peak: July-Aug.
BEANS,LIMA	year-round * peak: July-Oct.	CRANBERRIES	Sept.-Jan. peak: Nov.
BEETS	year-round peak: May-Oct.	CUCUMBERS	year-round ** peak: May-July
BERRIES: BLACKBERRIES DEWBERRIES LOGANBERRIES	April-Sept. peak: June	CURRANTS	June-Aug. peak: July
BLUEBERRIES HUCKLEBERRIES	early May-late Sept. peak: July	EGGPLANT	year-round peak: July-Sept.
GOOSEBERRIES	May-Aug.	ENDIVE AND ESCAROLE	year-round peak: Aug.-Oct.
RASPBERRIES BLACK AND RED	mid April-early Nov. peak: July	FIGS	June-Oct. peak: Aug.-Sept.
STRAWBERRIES	Jan.-July peak: May-June	GARLIC	practically year-round
BROCCOLI	year-round peak: Oct.-March	GRAPEFRUIT	year-round *** peak: Oct.-May
BRUSSELS SPROUTS	Sept.-March peak: Nov.-Jan.	GRAPES	June-Feb. **** peak: Aug.-Oct.
CABBAGE	year-round peak: Oct.-May	KALE	year-round peak: Nov.-March
		LEMONS	year-round peak: May-July

BANANAS: All imported. Supply normally available the year round.

* Most supplies in winter are imported.

** Light supplies are imported during winter months.

*** Some supplies in summer months are imported.

**** Supplies March-May are imported.